Mi
My Entity experience

Larry Dale

Edited by Norman Oliver F.R.A.S.

Mi
My Entity Experience

Copyright © 2010 Larry Dale

Type Font: Times New Roman size 12 & 14
Language – English (U.S.A.)
Printed in the United Sates of America by
Createspace

ISBN 10: 1-4196-4484-X

Cover design by Larry Dale

Other titles by Larry Dale
Mi Mathematics
Mi Entity Experience Revisited

Preface
(original version)

Within the realms of strange phenomena there are many reported and alleged Contact cases. They range from Abduction to Time Lapse phenomena. Some victims have a history of being susceptible to strange phenomena while others have no previous experiences. I say 'victims' because quite often the 'contactee' has very little to show for the experience except maybe, considerable stress and anxiety. Friends and relatives may even shun them. In addition to this, the so-called 'scientific community' often discredits or ignores such people because the scientist is often faced with 'un-measurable' and unknown quantities.

Thus these 'contactees' are not only victims of the phenomena, but also become victims of prejudice from other people. It is little wonder that some do not mention the event until many years later or even at all. Some decide not to relate their experience because they are afraid for their jobs and their reputation.

Many years ago I was once going to be on TV as part of a programme about astronomical anomalies, and the final part was to include UFO's. I spoke to some of the programme members who all basically denied believing in the phenomena. I asked if they did not believe, why include the topic of UFO's at all? "Don't you want to be on TV?", one asked. If I was to give details of certain selected events in an objective setting, then yes I would like to go on TV. However, if the idea was to give information solely for the purpose of 'explaining it away' as rubbish, then no, I did not want to go on TV.

In addition, I told them that one of them was not telling the truth, since one had already reported seeing something unusual. They all looked at each other, rather speechless, I might add. Needless to say I was not included in the programme.

I mention this for two reasons. One is that it was assumed I wanted a little bit of 'fame' that the medium of TV could offer. The assumption was wrong. Secondly, it brings out a type of arrogance that can infect people. Also, knowing one of them had lied about something that might be connected to the programme, what else might they lie about? More importantly it showed me just what these people thought about those of us who are chosen or struck by strange phenomena.

I might add here that Radio people seemed to be more interested in the phenomena and I always received a lot of respect from Local Radio.

A third reason for mentioning this is that I had hoped that ideas were radically changing from the previous misguided view. Alas, I think not. Though the details are omitted the latter parts of this book relate to certain mathematical ideas. Because some of these ideas are new, as far as I know, I wrote e-mails to certain Mathematical Societies for their advice. Although I did not disclose the Contact Experience itself, I did explain where basically some ideas had been derived from. To say that there was little interest is an understatement. In several cases I only got an automatic response such as "I am out of the office until........." but received no further replies. In one case I was told that if what I had derived was from other than a basic mathematical formulation, I was better off contacting an Astrologer, since they have an interest in 'meta-science'. This view is tantamount to saying that science only comes from science, which of course is a fallacy. Science comes from curiosity.

I would like to add that I have nothing against Astrologers. Indeed, they attempt to explain ideas where many scientists fear to tread.

So I decided that a personal publication was probably the best route to go for some of the ideas in this book, and I approached Norman Oliver for his advice. Not only was his advice sought for Norman was involved anyway because he has one or two of his own strange experiences to relate. Norman agreed that a publication by us seemed the best way to go.

In this book there are some experiences and coincidences that come prior to what may be considered as the main experience. One prior experience may well be connected to the main one, whereas the others may or may not be connected. Afterwards, comes an 'analytical' work in which 'coincidences' abound, but from these 'coincidences', came a flourish of new material that gave me a deep feeling of enlightenment when uncovered.

Preface

The material ranges over our three basic sciences, Mathematics, Physics and Chemistry. Since neither Norman nor I are responsible for the names, allocations and properties contained within these three, surely any coincidence of these with the experience must be viewed with interest. In this volume I have only mentioned the numerical coincidences, but have omitted their detail and derivation. These details are to be included in another book.

I would never have thought about the new material had it not been for the main 'character', Mi (pronounced 'mee') and some of my previous thoughts and ideas are now changing because of the experience.

Dates, concerning the experience have been used where possible, though many dates have been lost due to three main factors.

One is that here in Udornthani, Thailand, flooding has occurred each year and the extra building precautions that were made after the flooding of 2000 turned out to be grossly inadequate, The flooding of August 2001 was much worse than expected, and many files were lost.

Secondly, after transferring many e-mails to floppy disc I found that my computer became infected with computer viruses. After upgrading the computer, although I could delete the virus from my floppy discs many files were still inaccessible, and could not be 'opened' by the Word programme.

The third reason? Please read on and you will find out.

I would also like to inform the reader that my consumption of alcohol has never been to excessive levels, and for many years now I have been teetotal. I have never taken drugs for the sole purpose of enhancing my performance or just for the experience and, on occasion, I have refused those prescribed for illness. I have not smoked cigarettes for thirty-five years.

I want to thank Norman Oliver for his invaluable help and concerted efforts. Norman is also the editor of this book. I feel connected to Norman now, in such a way that I no longer see him as just a friend. Mi has given the bond between Norman and I a new meaning. Without Norman's involvement I am certain that I

Preface

would be sitting at home, a finger to lip, and wondering what the hell had happened. It thus goes without saying that this book about Mi would not have been produced had it not been for Norman.

It is my hope that any other person who has 'suffered' some strange experience, after reading this account will be given some satisfaction to know that there may a reason after all, for whatever was experienced.

Larry Dale F.R.A.S., January 2006, November 2007

Preface to the revised edition

After writing the third title Mi Entity Experience Revisited, I decided that the first, Mi, might be improved if the format was changed. However, this would entail considerable restructuring and the result could be a different book altogether. There might also be a mismatch with page references in the second and third titles so I opted for some minor but important changes.

Firstly, page numbers in the original were not inclusive and therefore broke with tradition and so the unnumbered pages have been deleted.

Secondly, the format has been changed slightly by deleting many of the computations involving Arithmetic and replacing them with an asterisk '*' marker. This marker informs the reader that the arithmetic has been inserted at the end of a section or chapter, enclosed in a 'box' marked with an asterisk. Appropriate wording containing the essential information replaces the deleted arithmetic and the 'boxed' arithmetic can be ignored by the reader who is not interested in the numerical details.

However, no changes have been applied to the diagrams illustrating the entity's answer to my two mathematical questions. In the explanatory pages I have retained the formulae given in the original version for the following reasons; a) to write each formula out in normal text format would probably result in confusion because of continuous references; b) since the diagrams represent an important part of the experience I want to convey, as much as

Preface

possible, my condition and position at the time the entity was in communication with me.

Larry Dale F.R.A.S. August 2010

FOREWORD

Having known Larry now for some thirty-five years since he and I first met as Council Members of BUFORA – The British UFO Research Association, there is only one thing I can say about the events he describes in these pages. That is – whatever he says happened in his 'MI' encounters and 'discussions' DID happen in the way he describes it. As BUFORA's NIC – National Investigations Coordinator – for a number of years, he always expected a very high standard from the investigators under his jurisdiction and was meticulous in the accuracy of his own investigations. The reader may take it for granted therefore that his description of the various occurrences related herein are as accurate as they could possibly be. The interpretation of these occurrences – and, indeed, the purpose behind them is obviously open to discussion and analysis as, indeed, is the origin of the entity – MI.

Larry and I conducted exhaustive enquiries and explored many avenues in endeavoring to uncover both the intentions of this entity and "his/its" location in the general scheme of things. Having considerable mathematical skills, Larry has largely focussed in this direction. As my own skills in the area are far less than Larry's I have tended to examine different facets of the situation and seek to establish an overall 'common denominator' without, perhaps, the greatest of success! Indeed, basically, as with the Montauk events – first publicized by Preston Nichols and Peter Moon – referred to herein, which may well have considerable relevance, this book is not only concerned with aspects of Time. It is also about Synchronicity, not just as in how, when and why occurrences and personal references are synchronistic, but mathematical and numerological synchronicity as well, though the latter are not presented in this volume. As with many other 'out of this world' experiences, maybe you, the reader, are the best person to judge the overall intention.

Norman Oliver F.R.A.S.   May 16th. 2005

Contents

Contents

Contents

III

Part 1 – Chapter 1 – The Beginning

I was christened Lawrence William Dale. My family used two shortened names for me, Larry and Lawrie. Another nickname was Lal. I was born in the district of Poplar in the East End of London on December the 8th 1942. Across the street in which I lived until the age of 14 were houses that showed the marks of bombing from the 2nd World War. Almost opposite my home remained the ruins of what was called Churchill Hall. In the house where I lived – one in a row of conjoined homes – there was another family. The parents had three children whereas I was an only child. They lived 'downstairs' and I lived 'upstairs'. There was a small yard at the rear in which we grew tomatoes and other vegetables, and these were separated or sectioned, using the corrugated iron sheets from the air raid shelter.

I can remember using the central flower area as a training spot for long jumping when I was preparing for a sports day at school. This little plot belonged to the other family and I was scolded many a time for endangering its existence. As it turned out its existence was fated anyway.

Adults, and the husband of the youngest daughter, occupied the next place along the street. The husband worked in one of the laboratory sections at the Kemball and Bishop Chemical Factory. With encouragement from my neighbor, at the age of 10 and 11 I became very interested in chemical ideas and it wasn't long before I began experimenting. Myself and the boy 'downstairs', who was almost the same age as me, would quite often go to the local park and try out some new mixture using model boats.

'JET X' fuel tablets were around at that time and these would be ground down to a powder and mixed with some other ingredients. The result was often of little motive power but it did create great volumes of smoke, which, of course, annoyed other pond users. We thought that the water was taking up most of the energy, and not being very good 'sailors' anyway, we graduated to flight. I had accumulated quite a large collection of Meccano pieces and we used them for making take off ramps for our rockets.

These 'rockets' were basically a tube from a well-known cigar brand. On the screw type cap we fixed small wooden spinning tops, which being pointed, would act as a streamlining

Chapter 1 – The Beginning

effect. A single hole or an arrangement of holes would be the exhaust exit. Everything was noted for future reference.

The tubes though, would distort and melt with the heat generated by the combustion and therefore they were not capable of being reused. I recall going to a boating pond with some friends armed with several of these tubes, with various modifications. One modification was a pin protruding from the spinning top point so that we could launch a 'boat tube' on the pond at a floating target board. While the board remained undamaged, the same could not be said for the small two-seater canoe, which rode into the path of two launches. I don't think the quality of the canoe could have been very good because it sank rather quickly behind a 'poof' and considerable smoke. The occupants decided to 'disembark' to safety.

Other incidents involved such occasions as the parachute jumping practice from a Barrage Balloon by the armed forces at another East End park and the disappearance of a friend's new bicycle, on which he hoped to break some speed record with the aid of a rather large rocket tube. There was always too much smoke to see what really happened.

My team-mate decided that we should launch from the upstairs window ledge and I would 'supervise' the mission. The result was that his mother's best scarf was ruined, my kitchen window was blown out, and he lay, very dazed, on the small grass verge below.

On the final occasion, which was to be a step for all boy-kind, we constructed an 18-inch rocket. With help from others, fuel containers inside were made and fins welded to the outside. We were supposed to wait until we went to the park, but being too impatient and inconsiderate, we could not wait to launch, and did so in the back yard. The rocket shot up to about the height of the house and then simply nose-dived right back down, straight into the central, nurtured bed of flowers. There was a flash; stones and soil showered our house as well as other surrounding places. The sound of breaking glass was all around us. We didn't mean to cause so much trouble, but the old couple in the opposite garden thought that World War 3 had begun. The damaged flower plot in

Chapter 1 – The Beginning

the center of the yard was never replanted after that and I never made any more rockets.

These beginnings showed where my inclinations were already pointing. Then there came a twist.

My father had a friend who was an officer in the Church Lads Brigade (C.L.B.). This was a Christian Movement in which the aim was not only to teach the Bible but also to train members in the ways of the Military. Many boys at that time turned to the Boys Brigade, which had naval inclinations, and their uniforms reflected this, the hats and badges being of Sailor design. The C.L.B. on the other hand, reflected a much stricter regime in that the uniforms were of heavy material, being composed of a tunic and trousers, with many brass colored buttons. The boys were expected to keep everything in tiptop condition and points were awarded when 'on parade' to keep track. These points would go towards an examination total for candidates who were interested in promotions. The Tunic had the stiff upright type of collar and I remember this as being very uncomfortable during the middle months of the year. The caps followed a traditional formal military style and were stiff. This, of course, was all part of the discipline training.

Bible and Church classes were aimed at people wishing to take Holy Communion and to be confirmed in the High Church of England. Similar to the Roman Catholic religion, the High Church of England held Mass, although there were distinct differences in the procedure, the main one being that a lot of the Mass was spoken in English and not in Latin.

My father's friend had also travelled while in the Forces and had been influenced by Middle Eastern techniques, particularly in the Martial Arts. With the help of both my father and his friend I was given instruction in certain mental techniques which included Meditation.

Like other members of the C.L.B. I was being prepared for Confirmation, being confirmed by the Bishop of Stepney in the East End of London. It was at this very time that another twist took place. Up until then I had been a believer in the faith, but I can remember quite clearly that the very moment the Bishop laid his

Chapter 1 – The Beginning

hand on my head became the very moment that serious doubt entered my thoughts. Instead of being happy about Confirmation, as were the many others on that day, I refused to go to the evening festivity. I began a deep thought routine, and it was many days before I attended meetings of the C.L.B. or Sunday Church. Eventually I went to Confession where I explained why I had been absent. It was then suggested to me that true faith was difficult to find and each of us should search for our own interpretation. I never returned to the Church, or to the C.L.B., became happy in the thought that there was something very fascinating about the universe and began reading books on Astronomy. I still practiced Meditation and continued to train in the Martial Arts where I hoped that the answers and enlightenment I sought would be in this direction.

After approximately a year, at the age of 13 and well into athletic training at school, something strange happened to me on the way to Grove Hall Park. This park was not far from where I lived, and very close to the Secondary Modern school (Fairfield Road) that I went to. This park and Victoria Park, were the two main places I would visit to train.

Around midday on a clear Saturday (either the last one in May or the first one of June) with both my mental and physical conditions similarly so, I approached the main Bow Road. Here I would cross the road and reach the central reservation. This central reservation was, and still is, a church-island, and divided Bow Road into a dual carriageway. On crossing the eastbound section suddenly everything slowed up. I was walking in a slow-motion type of way and remember trying very hard to walk normally – it seemed to take ages. Then on turning right, but looking left without knowing why, I saw 'another Larry' walking away to the left. Though there must only have been a look of sheer surprise on my face the 'other Larry' was smiling back.

Suddenly, everything was back to normal, but my increased effort propelled me forward at a rate faster than before and I collided with a lady carrying shopping bags. As soon as she finished making understandable remarks about the younger generation I rushed off to the left in search of the 'other Larry' but

Chapter 1 – The Beginning

was unsuccessful. When I related this to my friends, they shed tears of laughter.

Though no other mysterious events took place for the next few years, I always wondered about that one. Meditation never shed any light on the matter and I did not connect it to anything.

After marrying, and living in Winchester for about eighteen months, we returned to London and lived next door to my wife's parents. This close proximity had its problems, and when the opportunity arose to move to Kent, we did so. However, a short time after my wife's family followed. We now had a family of our own but earlier problems became intensified. I found I was unable to solve certain problems and spent more and more time in meditation in the hope of maintaining some mental perseverance. It was to my dismay that I found myself in conflict and felt alienated from my own family. The final result was that I spent three months in a psychiatric ward for what may be loosely termed a 'mental breakdown'.

In truth, it was the break that I needed but was unable to choose personally, and it removed me from the problem, at least temporarily. The doctors thought that hospitalization was not appropriate, because my problem hardly ranked with those of most of the other patients. However, along with my abilities it was considered that a little help was necessary, and that they might be able to provide explanations to my family where I seemed unable to do so. So ended this unpleasant episode and I did not allow myself to be overcome by such things again.

After securing a good job in a laboratory of the Schweppes Company in July 1973 (which lasted until early retirement in 1995) the next few years were without incident.

Then, early one evening when the children were in bed and my wife and I were looking at T.V............................

Chapter 2 – The Crying

We lived on a Council estate at St.Mary Cray in the district of Orpington, Kent, in a three bedroom house with the lounge, or living room, facing the street, the kitchen at the rear connecting to a reasonable sized garden. There was also a small garden at the front. There was no car parking space joined to the houses and cars had to be parked on the road. On one side was a family of four – two parents and two grown boys. On the other side there was a middle-aged family of three – a husband and wife and a brother of the husband. Our house was semi-detached with the family of three, but also joined on the other side with the front bedrooms sharing an adjoining wall. Beneath this was an arched passageway to the rear gardens. The stairway inside was on the side of the middle-aged family of three.

It was during this period that I joined BUFORA (The British UFO Research Association) and eventually became its N.I.C. (National Investigations Coordinator). During this time, I worked closely with Norman, who was Editor of the BUFORA Journal, on sighting reports. Norman's considerable experience and objective attitude as well as his lecturing expertise made him a very valuable person within the Association.

During the first half of August 1978 (my youngest daughter was three years old) when settling down for the evening, the children in bed, I was sitting in my usual place close to the lounge door. My wife would have been sitting on the opposite side facing the TV set. The TV set was on the same side as the lounge front window.

We were watching the programme that came before the late evening News, when I got up without saying anything and went upstairs. On returning just a few moments later I again said nothing and returned to the chair. After another few seconds I did a repeat performance, only this time on returning to the lounge, made a body gesture indicating some confusion. My wife asked me what I was doing and replied that I could hear one of the children crying, but that on reaching the top of the stairs the crying had stopped. Not needing to, I did not venture in any of the bedrooms and simply returned to the lounge. My wife remarked that she did not hear anything. This time I left the lounge door wide open where

Chapter 2 – The Crying

previously it had been only slightly ajar. Jennifer was the youngest and often woke up.

Then the crying came again, and my wife repeated that she could hear nothing. This time I walked slowly up the stairs; I found that the crying was loudest at about midway. As I moved upward the sound decreased. I put my ear to the wall, thinking that next door had visitors and maybe a baby was among them. I heard no sound coming from next door, and in fact they were not at home, but I didn't know that at the time.

The crying sound was not a full cry but more of a lengthy sobbing, and I heard this again a few times in the coming weeks until the latter half of September. On hearing it again I would investigate outside the house, both front and rear, and I checked the loft also. Each time the crying was loudest at about the middle of the stairway.

By this time my wife was becoming very angry and upset at my actions, and it was shortly after this I contacted Norman to ask whether he had any knowledge of this type of phenomenon. Norman made arrangements for me to meet with Timothy Good, who I went to meet sometime afterwards in Bromley, Kent. It was Tim's opinion that someone or something was trying to contact me, since having young children a crying sound would quickly get my attention. That was the end of the crying episode and I did not hear it again.

A couple of years afterwards we moved to the other side of the estate, St. Pauls Cray, to a house which faced the Petts Wood residential estate. At the continued request of my wife, I very reluctantly resigned from BUFORA. My father had died some years earlier and my mother died about this time also.

My wife was a Nursing Assistant at a Terminal ward and after returning home from an evening shift around 11.30/midnight she found that the children and I were in bed. I had to get up about 5 a.m. to go on the early shift. However, during the early hours something told me that I had to go downstairs. I wasn't sure what woke me, but everyone else remained undisturbed.

I slowly opened the living room door, the living room being a 'through' room, and without entering put my hand up to the right

Chapter 2 – The Crying

and turned on one of the lights. I listened but could hear nothing. I pushed the door wide open to the left and there in front of the TV set to the left and diagonally opposite, was a full size, transparent image of my father. His eyes were bulging as though when angry, but there was no movement or sound. I could see the TV and the wall behind quite clearly through the image but as soon as I took a step towards the image it immediately disappeared. Stepping backwards turning to see if anything was behind me and then checking that the image had not appeared again, I switched the light off and went back to bed.

It was time to go to work but I went into the living room to check and on the TV set was a potted plant, which had not been there the night before. Nor had I seen it when I saw the transparent image of my father. My wife was awake and she came downstairs and I told her what had happened to me during the early hours. She immediately picked up the potted plant and threw in the waste bin outside. One of the patients she had been nursing died during her shift and the plant had belonged to the patient.

The reason that I remember the date, 12th August, is that I remember remarking it happened half way between my son's birthday, 7th August, and my father's birthday on the 17th though strictly speaking I saw the image in the early hours of the 13th. However, my wife did bring the plant pot home on the 12th.

After this, there seemed to be some deterioration in the marriage but whether this had anything to do with my experiences is impossible to say. Certainly my wife felt very uncomfortable about things that were out of the ordinary. Eventually there was a divorce and soon after I met my second wife. This was a stormy marriage and lasted for only four years.

Late in 1991, with a girlfriend, I decided that I would fulfill a long ambition and take a holiday trip to China. As a Martial Artist and long associated with Oriental methods and ideas, China represented a link with techniques of searching for one's inner self. This holiday took place in 1992.

During these years, Norman and I kept in contact. It was late 1993 when the first of the 'coincidences' occurred. After coming home from Tae-Kwon-Do training I was in the house

Chapter 2 – The Crying

alone. I often did a meditation session after training mainly to relax and sometimes to concentrate on whatever techniques I thought necessary to think about. After one of these sessions I did not feel at ease and felt that there was more to life than just earning money and working weekend overtime. There was something 'nagging' at me but I could not uncover what it was. With my feelings at a high I threw my arms in the air and said 'Mum, tell me what to do'.

Norman knew of my girlfriend, but also knew that it was far from ideal and four or five days later I received a letter from Norman suggesting that if interested, I could be introduced to his Thai sister-in-law. Having split up with my girlfriend (again), I contacted Norman almost immediately and accepted the idea of an introduction by letter. Norman invited me to go and stay with him for a couple of days at the time of the New Year, and it was here that a second 'coincidence' happened.

I asked Norman for some details about the sister-in-law and it was then I found out that the lady had the same birth date as my mother, 23rd of January. [It is interesting to note here, that from my birthday there are 23 days to the end of the year.]

Norman himself was preparing to go to Thailand, though this time it was for a longer stay than before. He had a cat named 'Bimbo' and my cat was named 'Cassius' but as both cats were males they would probably end up trying to kill each other, I expressed disappointment at not being able to take care of Bimbo. Norman felt very upset about leaving his cat, but a short time after this Cassius died, whereby I was able to take care of Bimbo.

Once again this seemed very 'coincidental'. I took care of Bimbo until I took early retirement and left for Thailand on Saturday April 8th 1995, exactly 34 years to the day after my first marriage on April 8th 1961. Bimbo was given to a family in the West Country.

Norman and I first met when I joined BUFORA in the early 1970's, and now by marriage, we were brothers-in-law. A situation that I am sure both of us would have found amusing if we had been told years before that this was going to happen. However, as we shall see later, the acronym letter count for BUFORA and the name count for 'Thailand' produce several coincidences.

Chapter 2 – The Crying

I had not often thought of the earlier experiences in my third marriage since this was going to be a brand new beginning. I was going to live in a country that contained many things close to my own ways. I would not even have to worry about changing driving style since in Thailand they drive on the left, the same as in England. Having received my Tae-kwon-do Black Belt in England I began teaching in Udornthani, now my hometown. What also seemed strange to me was that I would also teach meditation to my students, which seemed rather like that old English saying of 'taking coals to Newcastle'.

Norman returned to England and divorced, whereby the brother-in-law aspect was dissolved, though we kept in touch. However, it seemed that once again we were separated. I have never doubted my decision to live in Thailand and recall as though it was only yesterday, stepping out of the train at Udornthani, feeling that 'this was it'. It already felt like home yet I had never been here before.

No unusual events took place until the New Millennium. Then, to quote my e-mail to Norman 12-2-2000:

"[referring to the first 'crying']...*until a couple of weeks ago. I have now heard it recently for three times – at night when I am asleep. I cannot hear the crying outside the bedroom but when I walk back into the bedroom I can hear it again. The crying lasts for about five minutes and then stops.........*"

I heard the 'crying' again on March 7th and March 25th. I already knew that there were no babies in any bungalow close enough to be heard this way. On the nights in question I would cautiously open the door and walk a couple paces outside the bedroom, where I could no longer hear the crying. As I looked back and returned to the bedroom, I noticed that my wife had not stirred.

On March 25th it was about noon that I heard the crying, while I was moving around in the bedroom. Walking towards the (shut) door and a point was reached where the crying seemed to be at a peak level; I turned and stood at that point. This time there was a tingling sensation all over and I suddenly saw what looked like a face, though it had characteristics that were unknown to me (see

Chapter 2 – The Crying

Figure En.1). The image did not illuminate the room yet I could see details very clearly with the bedroom curtains closed [the bedroom curtains are always kept closed] and the room in darkness. Because of this I wondered whether I was really looking at an image, or if the image was being projected into my mind. So the image may well have been a mental one.

I experienced very strange feelings, and it felt like things were being put into my mind. A feeling about 'time' and a feeling about 'equation' are the two remembered items, though there was a lot more going on than just these. While there is no confusion about a feeling concerning 'time', a feeling about 'equation' is not readily understood. One might ask, "What equation?", "Equation about what?", "one equation or more than one?" etc. However these questions would simply not apply to the sensation. One possible analogy, though not perfect, might be to that of sitting on a bus. The bus stops to allow people to get on and one's position might be that of being unable to see the entrance or exit. One can feel the result of people getting on or off, but to ask how many and what kind of people they were or what they were wearing, would be meaningless. All that one could say is that "people got on and people got off".

How much time elapsed from the start of the crying to the fading of the image is also not known, though it seemed a very long time. I then fell asleep.

Though there was no evidence to suggest what mode of 'communication' was being used I do remember it as though something technological was happening. Surely if it had been some kind of Spirit or Ghost then such entities would have a more widespread effect, and not just concentrated in one small area.

The most striking feature of the entity was that there were two pupils in each eye. A series of 'dots' were in the mouth position, and two 'extensions' at the side. There was a lighter elongated central region.

It was late March and Norman would have to wait until his return from lecturing at a conference in Eureka Springs, America, before he could see a drawing of the entity. I tried to send a drawing via an e-mail attachment, but Norman was unable to view

Chapter 2 – The Crying

it. Yet before going to America, being so intrigued, he began searching his vast 'library' of UFO material for any incident that might include an entity with similar features. He was unsuccessful and mentioned that he would enquire while in America.

On the March 27th, Norman wrote an e-mail with the reference 'twin pupils', where I had previously written 'double pupils'. Norman's terminology turned out to be prophetic and important later.

Figure En.1

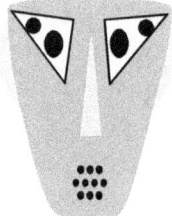

In the original colors the darkest area was a purple color, while the lighter central and side portions were bluish. What would be the whites of the eyes were a green color and the pupils black. The features were 'soft' and the whole seemed rather streamlined. Norman did find a UFO incident 18 months later that occurred in 1955 (see reference) that involved 'twin pupils'. However, in this case, the pupils were seen as one purple and the other green and were seen behind the visor of a helmet. No other facial features were noted. There was though, one point similar to the entity – the color of the pupils in the 1955 incident matched the colours noted with the entity.

One question in our minds was that, assuming that the crying on both occasions came from the same entity, why was there contact in Thailand and not in England? Was the entity unable to make contact in England? Did the entity therefore orchestrate my life so that I would go to Thailand? It was at this point that Norman was quick to point out the coincidence about my Thai wife's birthday and the coincidence concerning our cats.

Chapter 2 – The Crying

Obviously I was engrossed in the experience, but Norman had an equally strong curiosity. Before leaving for America on 6th April questions about past events and how the entity actually made contact flowed back and forth by email daily.

On returning from the conference, Norman wrote to me saying that no one at the conference could offer any assistance regarding the twin pupils.

Norman received drawings of the entity on the morning of Wednesday 3 May 2000 after his return.

The length of the 'head' is remarkable when compared to the 'face', and there is an 'overhead view'. Figure En.2 is their representation.

Figure En.2

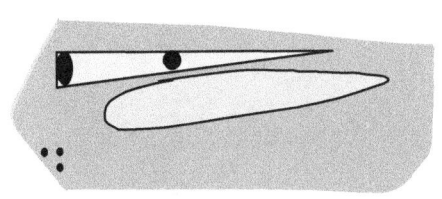 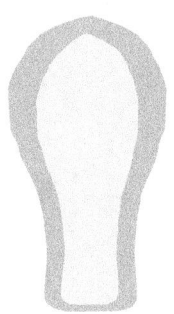

However these two views of the entity were not 'seen' in the same way as the original 'face'. One night I had a dream, in which the entity somehow took me on a type of tour, and I was floating around the original image. The colors were similar, except that for the overhead view, the interior was very bright. Though criticisms are leveled at believing the content of dreams, I felt there was good reason to suppose that the 'dreams' of the entity, were not just dreams, but 'thoughts' implanted by the entity during the time of contact. Moreover, no dreams about such an entity could be remembered prior to the experience.

The only thing that came into my mind about the shape of the overhead view was that of a tomb or coffin. On the 4th May I asked Norman what he thought the overhead view looked like, without having previously told him of my idea. In his exact words:

Chapter 2 – The Crying

'…to be honest, the FIRST thing that came into my head was a coffin (Sorry about that!)…'

I felt a kind of 'invitation' to go inside the overhead view but even in the dream I seemed to have some control over my direction, and there was a feeling of apprehension so I moved away from the bright overhead view. Why there was apprehension is a little mysterious, because, as indicated in the appearance of my father's image, I tend to move toward things that are of a curious nature. Instinct here suggested a retreat. The 'floating' motion was unusual too, in that there was firmness and a feeling of support, though nothing visual was noted.

Reference. The Rae Fountain Affair by Margaret Fry 1978

Chapter 3 – Where I had not gone before

The crying did not occur again nor was the image seen, and I had the feeling that now it was 'my turn' to try and make contact. How I should try to make contact with the entity was uncertain, since no instructions were mentioned.

The first thing that came to mind was Meditation. Having had considerable practice thought I would try to uncover anything useful. In addition to that it was becoming obvious that some stress, in the form of extreme curiosity, was creeping in and meditation might help remove it. An interesting note here is that my 'meditation color' is purple.

So, starting with the 'guide' form, I began meditating, but no matter how I tried I just could not get into my usual routine. Finally, having successfully entered some kind of entrance, I found that what was before me was a screen with the entity's image on it. It became obvious that I was not going to be allowed to proceed until I had done some appropriate thing.

I asked about the identity of the entity, to which came the reply 'Me', although this could be written 'Mi' or even 'Mee'. Another question was whether or not the entity was human and the answer was 'No'. To the question about the whereabouts of the entity the answer was to say the least, teasing, 'can everywhere to 24'. It seemed to me at this point that not only was there some kind of language problem, since the answer 'can everywhere to 24' could hardly be considered good English, but it also meant something else far more important. The answers were obviously not a *mental meaning or thought transfer* since this would not require a specific language. So it meant that the entity was fallible. It is also true to say that I did not 'hear' the answers either. Rather more like a kind of insertion.

To avoid confusion I chose the spelling 'Mi' and this turned out to be prophetic. [I now believe that I was influenced by Mi to spell the name this way.]

The color of the image was green, but at each answer given there was a slight change to a shade of purple. Only a frontal view of the image was seen. Sometimes I would ask a question but not get an answer, though now, it is impossible to say what those questions were. When I received an answer the image slowly

Chapter 3 – Where I had not gone before

disappeared and I was allowed to continue my mental journey until meeting the image again. Throughout the coming weeks this type of session was repeated until the last few days of June.

When restarting Meditation I always had to start at the beginning and not simply begin where the previous session ended. It seemed that previous answers could be revisited but only up to a limit, after which I was unable to do so.

During the question and answer sessions, ideas about Time were 'discussed' and it seemed that Mi considered our ideas about Time as being wrong, or at the very least, needed adjustment.

As an example:-

Most people are aware that a flowing electrical charge will produce an accompanying Magnetic Field. Indeed, this is one reason why transmission cables have insulation. It was also a reason for telephone interference in the old cable systems of thirty or forty years ago. Mi stated that associated with Electrical and Magnetic fields was also a Time field and that this was different to the *passage of time* that we might use to count during of the flow of the current. Mi also seemed to imply that the Time field was more associated with the Magnetic field than with the Electric charge.

In the diagram on the next page I try to give a representation of this idea, though it should be understood that there was more to this, the nature of which I did not clearly understand.

(Continued on page 18)

Chapter 3 – Where I had not gone before

Diagram T.1 showing the Electromagnetic field and the suggested Time field.

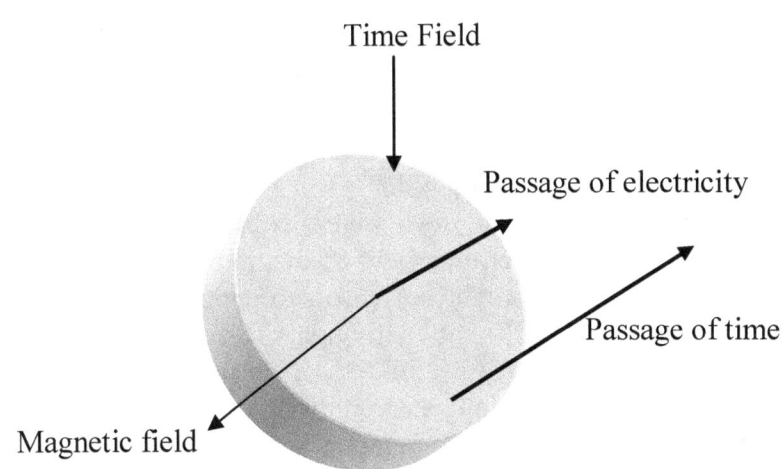

Chapter 3 – Where I had not gone before

A Time field associated with Electromagnetic fields is not really an extreme view and it could explain much about apparent current anomalies. There are very few people who have not heard of the ill-fated Philadelphia Experiment where scientists tried to initiate an invisibility shield. If there was a Time Component there, which was not reckoned for, then this might account for some of the alleged phenomena.

However, it seemed quite obvious that Mi was convinced of the existence of another Time aspect. To Mi, our version of Time was no more than a historical reference system, where each second, hour and day went by and we had no other definition concerning this progression. It is rather like travelling on board a train where the passengers do not see the driver and have no idea as to what kind of person the driver is. This is just my analogy and I don't think we can stretch it too far

There are some more of Mi's ideas connected to Time later in this chapter, from which the view of diagram T.1 needs to be modified a little. There might be reason to suppose that Mi has given us some valid information though. This experience took place five years ago, yet in April of 2002 there was much publicity about certain inventions being patented that use magnetic fields for anti-gravity effects. It should be remembered that Albert Einstein, in his equations of General Relativity, gave a connection between Time and Gravity.

'Time is not a *constant*', is a statement that you will find in books about Relativity, of which there are many popularized versions. However, although scientists today speak of Gravitons as being packets or quanta of Gravity, the basic definition of Gravity has not changed for many years. The definition is linked to that of anything possessing Mass. Time, as we define it, is affected by Gravity, and Gravity appears to have a singular effect, that of attraction. Is it possible that Gravity is a more fundamental part of Time? Would this not connect with present day experiments such as that mentioned above?

We now return to the experience and the procedure.

I had to arrange my questions where I thought I might get an idea of how Mi life thinks or comprehends its surroundings, and

Chapter 3 – Where I had not gone before

thought that a question involving numbers or equations might be a direct route to this. I thought that asking questions about an 'almighty' or divine being would not be very useful since it would still be a matter of one's own beliefs in proving whatever answer was given.

At this point, it is worth a mention that our numerical system is an abstract system that is capable of making certain predictions about our environment. I will have more to say about this later on. I wanted to know if, within the Mi life knowledge, there was a number system similar to ours and if so, how it was organized.

The short answer to the question of numbers was "no", Mi life does not use numbers. How was I going to ask questions, since our counting system only used numbers? I decided to ask questions involving numbers anyway, since any result might be interesting. Unfortunately, the first set of answers seemed to be in the form of pictures and geometrical objects that were not all understood by me because they all had some additional property that seemed incomprehensible

I thought that maybe I should make the questions very simple and thus any answer might be easier to relate or translate.

I asked the question, if x plus y equals 3, and x minus y equals minus 1, what are the values of x and y. (This is called a 'simultaneous equation in two unknowns'). Although I cannot give a complete and accurate description of Mi's answer, the basic essentials are there.

I thought that this was quite simple and should step up a gear so to speak, expecting a similar pattern in the answer. In the previous question there were two 'unknowns', x and y: the next question involved three 'unknowns' a, b and c. The question was:-
If

$$3a + 4b - 2c = 4$$
$$5a + 2b + 3c = 10$$
$$4a - 3b + 4c = 15$$

Chapter 3 – Where I had not gone before

what are the values of *a*, *b* and *c*? Mi's solution was nothing like the previous one and most definitely not as easy to understand. I spent considerable time working through this one with Mi's guidance, though Mi's assistance was minimal. This might have been a deliberate ploy by Mi to remove the 'cobwebs' out of my mind.

In Chapter 10 I revisit these questions and try to explain Mi's representations of these questions. (Just in case you are interested, $a = 3.2$, $b = -1.8$, $c = -0.8$)

Further questions were related to other ideas, for example, that of Time. As far as I was able to understand, Mi's idea of Time was very different from our own. In terminology that may not be completely accurate, Mi communicated ideas of 'Active' and 'Passive' Time. According to Mi, Now and the Past belong to Active Time while the Future is Passive Time. This might mean that in some way the areas of Now and the Past have become 'activated' while the Future remains 'Unactivated'. However, in addition to these three, Mi communicated the idea of a fourth Time area which also belonged to Passive Time. I can only loosely identify this as 'Unused' Time. This non-active Time can permeate the other three mentioned and also be external to them. Each of the four has a different 'signature', though this is capable of change and indeed does change, and it is this signature that is the 'Flowing' element of Time. As one might expect, these ideas were not immediately acknowledged or understood by me.

Mi gave a three-part definition as follows: -

The Fundamental Fabric of our (not Mi's) Universe is a General Time Component (G.T.C).

A General Operating Time Component is composed of two or more G.T.C.'s.

A Special Operating Time Component is the second part of the above with a functional anomaly.

Chapter 3 – Where I had not gone before

It needs to be understood that this definition is in my words, which was the best I could do at the time; I was concerned about using the term 'functional anomaly'. However, we might be able to distinguish between our ideas and Mi's ideas by saying Passage Time (ours) P.T., and Component Time (Mi's) C.T.

Everything has a unique C.T. signature

It was this fourth part that probably has a path to understanding the others but having said that, it also makes any Time field very difficult to visualize.

So, whilst parts 1,2 and 3 of Mi's definitions, if that is what we can call them, may be interesting, it may be part four that is the most provocative.

One provocative idea is this. If one had the sensory ability and assuming that the signature does not involve colors, one could live in a universe all one color yet still be able to distinguish between one item and another.

This is the final chapter that discusses the experience directly but a summary of what has been discussed so far might be useful and then end with some final 'comments' by Mi.

It is true that I had some history of strange phenomena, but then again, many people might lay claim to far more experiences. However, seeing an image of oneself separate and moving in an opposite direction is perhaps not so widely experienced. It also seems that to hear 'crying', is not an unusual experience either, but perhaps two events of 'crying' at about 24 years apart, is again, not so widely known. Experiencing an apparition of ones parents is a common occurrence, and the one related in this account has no claim to being more unusual than that of anyone else.

Perhaps the main difference with the experience of Mi is the information imparted by this entity. Indeed I maintain that certain items yet to be disclosed would not have been uncovered by me without having had the experience. Investigators of strange phenomena, and those involved in any follow up are always looking for something that would help to substantiate the witnesses' claims. The diagrams in the later chapters would, I

Chapter 3 – Where I had not gone before

think, not be considered as substantial evidence of any contact because they lack the all-important bridge of connecting our knowledge to that of another form of life. However, any lack of evidence within these is not the fault of Mi, but is through my own ignorance and inability to understand clearly what Mi was trying to communicate.

This brings us to an important question – why did Mi choose to contact me and not contact someone who was more intelligent? I am not a mathematician, but possess an appetite for the 'beauty' that sometimes can resemble that of a painting that may capture a magic moment of Nature. This was illustrated when trying to work through Mi's answers to the simple Simultaneous Equations. The numbers and the 'answers' from Mi seemed to fit, though it must be said that a lot more work needs to be done to completely understand Mi's set of three equations.

It seems Mi can identify properties of Time, which our definition excludes. It is true that we talk about the past, present and future, but we have no idea what actually is the difference. It is like firing a bullet at a target. There is very little thought about what the bullet is doing as it proceeds on its path, and once through the target, it is forgotten altogether. We are either glad we hit the center, or decide we need more practice. Sometimes a real expert comes along and his shooting is more consistent because he understands the nature of what is happening, and the gun is no longer a gun but an extension of himself.

Or another example: -

I once had the opportunity to talk to a very famous jockey, and asked what he thought separated him from the rest. His reply was enlightening.

'Most people think of riding the horse. I don't. I am part of the horse and we run together'

Is this how Mi views Time? Or more correctly, interacts with it?

Is this why Mi is incapable of considering 'nothingness'?

Mi was aware that I had done a lot of theorizing about trying to prove that absolute nothing cannot exist. Mi could not understand why I should do this when the answer is so self-

Chapter 3 – Where I had not gone before

evident. Mi also suggested that there was a connection between Human death and C.T.

Other remarks by Mi include the following: -

'.......in watering dark lagoons where the P.T. is of little consequence yet still it enters to sustain life.....'

The 'it' does not refer to P.T. but something else, though this is not made clear.

'........and as overhead you be why you found not to enter. You would not drown on the inner portion but you drift with it and it not wait for you.'

This is referring to the overhead view of the entity as shown in 'E' diagrams. It seems to have the same implication as that proverb about Time and Tide.

'.......in my first communication you were only aware of a lonely view yet until later you found a regal presence floating there to later still – is this not a connecting plane?'

Here the connection seems to be with the original 'face', or perhaps the first 'crying' that I experienced, though the reference to a regal presence is not clearly understood. It may refer to that which was experienced during meditating sessions.

It seems that at one point I was feeling somewhat fatigued and decided a little digression might help, so I asked a question of Mi about something not related to the previous questions. I asked about 'ball lightning'. It turned out that Mi had quite a lot to say about this type of phenomenon, so much so that after completion I felt much worse than before. There appears to have been some confusion about what I meant by 'ball lightning', but after sorting this out Mi had several points to impart to me.

Mi suggested that there are many phenomena that fit my description and where we have one general grouping for the phenomenon, Mi has a classification of two groups depending on their properties or origin. Mi states that while some are relatively harmless, others should definitely be avoided. Usually those that are produced from a 'domestic' situation are not harmful, while those from a 'foreign' high powered source can affect the locality where they are 'deposited'. Small round shapes moving in a circular motion which are very energetic can affect human

Chapter 3 – Where I had not gone before

perception and memory, according to Mi. My notes for this period did not contain much else by way of explanation.

These were answers, or part answers, to now-forgotten questions. Forgotten??? How could one forget such an experience?

In my e-mail of the 21st June 2000, I wrote:

"Communication with the 'Mi program' has been completed. I am not sure 'completed' is the right word, and the image is no longer with me"

Also in this e-mail there was mention of a dream about Buddha, with the image of Mi being present. People in the dream were saying that the usual position of Buddha with hands together was wrong. The place was Easter Island.

On the 8th of August I sent another e-mail to Norman saying that a strange thing had happened. All recall regarding the programme had been 'lost' and that apart from the copious notes, no memory remained. The 'memory loss' also appeared to have affected some Tae-kwon-do Patterns that I had been studying during the previous few weeks. Four out of the five Patterns were totally forgotten and needed to be studied over again, equivalent to about three weeks study. The final meditation session appeared to be one where some details of previous sessions needed some revisiting. A feeling of much apprehension was realized and I began to feel uncomfortable; there was a feeling of something 'behind' but I was unable to turn. In fact I was unable to do anything, and there was now a building up of anxiety. I decided just to try and relax. Suddenly a 'jolt' was felt and a feeling of having fallen over, but I was now able to open my eyes and saw that my position was upright.

These were Mi's final words as I'd written them down – "unable to respond".

'Many life has been like Man and Man will be like them – without the property of life and same as Dinosaurs. A Brain, the Brain is the same as the progress of the young one it must have food of the right type to develop rightly. The Brain of Man is young and if the food is right, will meet its destination. If the food is wrong Man will either die or be put to death.

Chapter 3 – Where I had not gone before

The Technology of any life must not outpace the brain of that life because this does to laziness and able to muscle fit but Brain will lose. Man may get Technology Brain and become two man types and so will make for less chance that Brain to become developed. Technology Brain can die easy without leaving its message.

The formula is that when Brain is developed faster than Technology that life will succeed. If Technology faster than Brain that life will die. Technology alone cannot escape the End Realism but the Brain alone can or Technology at the back of Brain can.'

Translation:- (Outside of quotes I assume here that I must have had some kind of reason or background knowledge for interpreting the way that I did)

"There have been many forms of life in 'our' universe that have been in a similar situation to Man on the Earth, but they have become extinct and Man will become extinct if Man does not change his course. The Human Brain will evolve but its evolution depends on the type of input it receives. If Man just concentrates on improving Technology, the Technology alone will not service the evolution of the Human Brain. The evolution of the brain must be a natural one so that life expectancy will improve as well. Technology will improve our leisure time and the Human race will be split into two parts – those having taken advantage of more leisure time to engage in some physical activity and those who take advantage of the mental applications of that technology (become more intelligent.)

Assuming all natural things allow, there are only two situations where man can escape extinction. We must not allow our technology to improve our technology. I am not too sure of the validity of 'Mi' here though this is the case in many computer applications where a computer actually designs the next step, but it would be wrong to suggest that we don't understand it. However, I do understand Mi's point.

If the evolution of both the Technology and the Brain are at equal rates, or the Brain is evolving faster than Technology Man will avoid extinction. It may be possible, as seen in some Science fiction movies, to enhance the Brain by using some technical

Chapter 3 – Where I had not gone before

device, but this is unstable and results will occur only in individual cases and not in Mankind in general.

We have faster and better 'space ships' but these will stay within our universe and if our universe suffers or ends then so will these. Mi seems to think that because these pieces of technology have a physical nature belonging to our dimension they will not be able to enter another dimension and escape misfortune. However, if Man's Brain (mind) is evolved enough, Man's Brain (mind) can escape the misfortune."

During the previous weeks I had written to Norman with notes that were called Med. Concepts (short for Meditation and Mi concepts), the final set of these, M/C.3 being sent a few days after the 'loss of memory'

Memory of the original Contact experience remained, along with the knowledge that there was a 'program'; the knowledge that it had gone, also remained. Continuous efforts in further meditation sessions revealed nothing about Mi.

The only thing that I can now remember is that on starting a meditation session no form of the image could be encountered. It seemed that the 'consultation' process was over. What was even more astonishing was that even the copious notes and drawings meant very little and I could not relate to them at all. I could remember having had an experience with Mi, and the original 'crying' episode, but that was all. No matter how I tried during meditation to recover items noted after sessions, the result was zero. It seemed that all had been 'deleted'.

This and the previous chapters have been written from notes and letters that passed between Norman and me during the period while the experience with the image was ongoing.

Though this has been the 'end' of the Mi experience, other, and what appeared to be unrelated strange occurrences, began (see later). However, it seemed that I was clearly now in a 'Post Mi' situation, feeling quite exhausted and in need of a rest.

One attitude did seem to remain with me, however. I felt a driving force, or thirst, to try to understand what had happened and in Part 2, you will see the fruits of our labors. I had the strong feeling that I had been contacted for a reason, but I was also

Chapter 3 – Where I had not gone before

mindful that it may have been nothing more than a 'prank'. For example a cat may think, 'Ouch. Why did that human tie a tin can to my tail?' I know this may be stretching things a little, but I am sure you see what I am driving at. Without evidence one way or the other, I assumed the former and you will read later Norman has some views on this. My feeling was that a challenge had been offered and if not picked up I would perhaps wonder what might have happened if I did.

In the weeks and months that followed it became clear that one 'coincidence' would lead to a string of others. A small number of dreams were unusually strong in nature and I would quite often wake in the middle of the night feeling as though my head was about to burst. In some dreams I would actually find the answer to certain problems, and would get up to write them down.

There developed some lengthy research correspondence between Norman and I. Apart from the Internet, I did not have access to historical records regarding certain ideas, because these were not available in Thailand. Not only did Norman become an essential link but it became obvious that he too was part of the experience. The reasons for this will be discussed later.

I was convinced that there had to be a meaning to the experience, and most of my spare time, sometimes into the early hours, would be spent trying to work things out. It soon became clear to me also, that something was 'afoot', and the drive to find out what became even stronger.

Before going on to these extensions, below are some of Norman's comments before reading what was the final MC/3.

"As maybe I've suggested before, to my mind the really puzzling thing has nothing to do with actual content: this is the question as to why MI takes a heck of a lot of trouble to contact you, then lets YOU ask the questions, which 'HE' may or may not decide to answer. It would therefore appear that it wasn't in order to impart any Earth-shattering (sorry!) info. about his planet, or himself, his race /whereabouts /intentions/ Earth etc etc., but just so that he could answer questions – seemingly any sort of questions other than those which would (naturally) request

Chapter 3 – Where I had not gone before

information about his/their physical/mental makeup and whereabouts.

Could it be, one wonders, that MI and others of his kind are randomly contacting Earth people for experimental purposes using different methods for different people? It need not have been the same 'MI' who tried the first 'crying child' contact. (MI could be a generic term for 'his' people. Can't recall offhand whether you dubbed him 'MI' yourself, – I rather think you did but, even if so, then the appellation could just have been put into your head anyway.) In any case, as I say, it need not have been the same 'MI' – it might just be that, for some reason, such crying was considered by those concerned to be the best way of attracting YOUR attention. There might be many different ways for other people.

What I'm suggesting, I suppose, is one of two things. Either (1) that it's part of a laboratory experiment with humans to examine reactions and mental capabilities or (2) part of a 'curriculum' in their equivalent of an educational institution, which could either be 'live' to participants or, in some way, recorded and 'played back' to a class. When the 'lecturer' thought he'd enough material to demonstrate a particular point or points or line(s) of research he would 'cut off' from you, having 'dialled' their equivalent of the English '141' which ensures his call can't be traced! Perhaps he could call his 'Course' something like 'Examination of Anomalous Alien Thought Processes'! Whatever, the key point to me is that it appears there was no specific reason to contact you other than to see what type of questions that you – as a subject – would ask. He would then tailor his replies accordingly – maybe for future replay after editing.

I'd tend to agree with MI that we've become lazy in developing our senses in many directions, but, I wonder, could not the same criticism be levelled at him (them) for 'taking an easy way'? From what you've written I'd consider that his/their 'empathetic' method of locating positions / describing shapes / numbers / fractions / positions could well be less precise than our own 'primitive' numerical / mathematical / geometrical / whatever systems. You probably can't now actually recall if you put it to him

Chapter 3 – Where I had not gone before

at any point that our system(s) might actually be better than his/theirs. Maybe you did, though, and MI took umbrage and ceased communication! Just a thought. Since you've lost actual recall of what transpired between you, in any case you'll only be able to check what was spoken of from what you've actually written down. Maybe previous experience with 'guides' may help, but might somewhere there just be an indication of some way whereby you might contact HIM? Maybe there could be and THAT was why recall was more or less erased. However, the way in which your experiences ended does just make me want to go back to the 'class demonstration' angle.

"Right, chaps, that's enough for this session – there'll be another subject's reactions for you to study tomorrow"! Just a thought about how your recollection of and 'conversations' with MI have/are being erased, so to speak. I'm not, of course, suggesting that you've dreamed everything up, but might there be a correlation between the way one's recollection of dreams disappears as one enters a waking state, which I often find frustrating, and your recollections of MI disappearing. Mind, there is a school of thought that considers dreams are actually our waking state and vice versa. Actually, when one thinks about it, it's not that dissimilar a thought to the 'What if we were actually in a black hole?'(A conception referred to in earlier correspondence.)

Yes, direction-wise, so to speak, I take the analogy of how to find where one's car is. It's rather like saying "turn down by the apple tree at the side of the Dog and Duck; go down to the Post Office then turn towards the Clock Tower and you'll see a shop which sells black puddings; then go down the alleyway at the side"! Certainly not as mundane as "First right, second on the left and it's straight in front of you!"

Anyway, Larry, I'll break off at this point. The foregoing is, as I say, purely an 'overview'. It barely touches any of the detail in M/C3 which I WILL endeavour to examine more closely in a later e-mail/letter, but I thought I'd get this off to you in the meantime."

As one can see there was a great deal of thought, research and correspondence, between us. At times my extension room

Chapter 3 – Where I had not gone before

would look more like a waste paper factory, with various notes scattered around regarding different lines of possibilities.

Once again I tried through meditation to see if there were any remnants of the 'program'. None were found. However, something else interesting had happened. One of my mental guides had been replaced or changed into what looked like some Egyptian Queen. She held a glass shape in her hands, which was purple in color. In trying to find out if the lady was an *authentic* guide, the answer received was that she was Queen of the Sea. The reason I thought she was Egyptian was that she was wearing garments that resembled those of a Queen or high ranking Egyptian female of the past. Around the neck she wore a 'Sun ray' design and a headset with a Sun decoration. She wore a long orange skirt, with a bird design on it, which hid the legs and feet.

However, after a lengthy search, apart from the Sun God Ra, and the daughter of the same being saved from the sea, no description of an Egyptian Sea Queen could be found.

There came a series of strange sightings. I taught Tae-kwon-do in the large Basketball hall in the main (Secondary) school in Udornthani, not far from where I live. One evening in September, while talking to one of my students, I noticed out of the corner of my right eye, a lone person sitting up on my right in the concrete spectator area. I turned my head and noticed that she was sitting quite naturally, dressed conventionally wearing a skirt, and appeared to be Thai. That is she had a tanned skin and long dark hair.

The Basketball hall is on the second floor and shown in the diagram on the next page. The two arrows on the left indicate stairways, while the top and bottom arrows on the right indicate the Basketball teacher's office and storeroom respectively. The second arrow down on the right shows the position of the stairway to the main entrance. The central rectangle is the game area while the two horizontal lines top and bottom, along with two vertical lines on the right, are elevated concrete seating areas. The black diamond shape on the left is my usual teaching position, while the two black rectangular shapes and the solid line arrows show the position of the lady.

Chapter 3 – Where I had not gone before

Lady

It is not unusual sometimes, for parents to come and watch their children, and I turned my head back to the student I was talking to. Then I quickly turned my head again in the direction of the lone lady, but she had disappeared. The distance that she would have to go to leave my view, in any direction, was great enough for me to have seen her moving. This happened again on another evening, only this time the lady was sitting facing directly opposite to me. I did not see her arrive, which would have been almost impossible, since I always use the same area for my position when teaching. I turned my head for a 'split second' and on looking back, the lady had again vanished. I asked some of my students who were moving in the lady's direction, and they simply replied ' Poo Ying Rheu, Mai Hen' which means that they did not see a lady. Coming or going they should have seen her, especially when considering the sideways distance involved.

Norman had also pointed out that the 'mysterious lady', as she had now come to be called by us, might be an introduction to a repeat of the Mi entity experience but as yet a repeat performance has not occurred. Then…

One night while my wife and I were asleep, I woke up with a 'start'. I turned slowly and there, lying beside me, was the 'mysterious lady'. I got up cautiously, but as I turned back she had vanished again, and I could see my wife clearly, asleep. When we got up the following morning my wife mentioned that she had a dream where a lady with long hair was lying between us (my wife keeps her hair on the short side). Because I did not want alarm my

Chapter 3 – Where I had not gone before

wife I did not, and to this day have not, mentioned this experience to her.

At a time when my wife's sister, Noi, was living with us, another strange event happened. I had been doing some computer work before going to teach Tae-kwon-do. After getting myself ready I crossed the living room and, noticing that Noi was sitting on the wooden settee, I went out without locking the front door. On my return Noi quickly confronted me asking why all the doors were left open when I went out. I explained why. Noi said that could not have been so because she had gone out about an hour prior to that. (As Norman will confirm this is a Thai trait. Members of the family do not feel it necessary to announce that they are going out, and come and go without a word. Indeed, they feel it is an infringement of their freedom if they have to say so). We both laughed about my explanation but I was thinking something else. I had not directly looked at the lady sitting on the settee, but remembered that she was sitting with her legs crossed wearing a skirt. I realized that Noi in fact never did wear a skirt and certainly never sat in that way. Whether it was the 'mysterious lady' or some other person just waiting I will never know.

The last time I saw the 'mysterious lady' was at a time when I entered the living-room from the kitchen. The wooden settee is diagonally opposite and there, with a nice smile on her face, was the mysterious lady, looking straight at me. Just as I was about to approach her, what seemed like a loud male voice from behind me shouted, " It's there right in front of you three hundred years ago." The voice spoke the words in a single tone and without punctuation, so there was no way of telling what the words meant. I instinctively turned my head to the rear and saw…nothing, and as I turned my head back again to look at the lady, she had vanished once more. Up to this time, I have not seen her again.

There were other strange happenings also. In the middle of the day, sometimes when others were present in the same room, I would be walking and suddenly with a flash I would find myself walking inside a ('ordinary') dream that I may have had the night before. I would take several steps before emerging from the dream and at the exact same spot that I entered. Other people present,

Chapter 3 – Where I had not gone before

such as my wife, made no comment, so I assumed they had not been aware that anything unusual had happened.

Though the mysterious lady was not seen again, a kind of 'blur' was frequently noticed. On many occasions I would be doing something quite unrelated to the experience, when out of the corner of my eye I would catch sight of a fast moving dark grayish blur. On one occasion it was seen moving from the front door into the bungalow, whereby the hanging curtain over Noi's bedroom door (directly opposite the front door), waved about as though it had been hit by a gale force wind. The blur appeared to be similar in shape to one that might be made on a piece of paper with a pencil, as in tracing out an article below the paper.

The occurrence of the blur seemed to diminish in frequency until it reached the point of being seen only once a month. The last occurrence was on Friday 1st of March 2002.

Around this period was the last time I saw the Mi image. This was in a dream, and was about England. I was standing on a balcony and I looked up and there was a log of wood moving downward towards me. Someone to my side said that it was the ghost 'eleet'(or elite, or elete...?) and that she wanted to talk to me. I had to duck out of the way to avoid being hit by the log. As I turned, the log had changed into the image of Mi. Our searches for someone called 'eleet' or variations thereof, were not successful.

Dreams about Norse or Viking mythology were very prominent and were extremely vivid. Having a conversation with Odin is not quite the usual thing to do! The themes of these dreams were about the Norse equivalent of Armageddon, Ragnarok, involving Odin, Thor and Loki. While I remembered some of this, Norman did most of the research on the topic.

Chapter 4 – JUST A FEW THOUGHTS
Norman Oliver

When I first read through and edited Larry's narration of the 'Mi' events, two thoughts came to mind. Firstly *"What can I contribute to these pages that hasn't been covered fully already?"* and secondly, *"My math isn't up to Larry's standard, so my best approach to events should be philosophical in nature rather than mathematical"*!

So, in this, the first of two chapters, the emphasis will be on my own background, particularly in relation to UFOs, Aliens, Cosmology and, indeed, what one might term 'The Unusual' in general, whilst the second will deal with suggestions, thoughts and ideas I consider may have some relevance to Larry's experiences – and possibly some of my own.

"Moon Broke" was an early remark I was alleged to have come out with around the tender age of two when, being wheeled around in a pushchair, I uttered these immortal words on seeing our closest planetary neighbour approaching its 'half' phase. So dinned into me was it subsequently, that I actually came to believe in later life I remembered uttering them!

This did, though, presage a strong interest in Astronomy in my formative years and I quickly ran through most of the books on the subject that were to be found in my local library – 'local' being the town of Worthing in West Sussex where I was born. World War II then came on the scene, resulting in an increase in my interest, as the enforced black-out enabled me to view the planets, stars and constellations with a clarity not previously to be enjoyed. *Vega, Altair, Aldebaran, Rigel* and the rest of the twenty or so first-magnitude stars became not just names, but friends in the summer and winter skies. Star clusters such as the *Pleiades, The Hyades*: the nebulae in *Orion* and *Andromeda* were able to be viewed with an awesome clarity. Gossamer-like, the Milky Way swathed its way through the constellations – a meandering river of subdued light.

The only really strange experience I can recall from my teens was wakening once in the middle of the night and finding that right and left were 'transposed' as it were, and I had to pinch myself to be convinced it was no dream. Instead of the bed being flush with the wall and having to get out of bed on the right, the

Chapter 4 – JUST A FEW THOUGHTS
Norman Oliver

right of the bed was against the wall and I had to alight from the left! Somewhat timorously I got up and stepped out to the landing – which again was spatially transposed. I was on the point of going downstairs to settle the matter when I grabbed the banister rail to assist my descent (stairs were steep in those days!), but, of course, with my wrong hand, and almost made an involuntary dive to the bottom. At this, I decided discretion was definitely the better part of valour and returned to my bed, still picking my way somewhat carefully, not knowing my left hand from my right, so to speak. On reaching the bed I hurriedly disappeared beneath the bedclothes, straight away fell asleep again and, lo, in the morning, right was right and left was left, just as they should be!

Near the end of World War II I was directed, not into National Service, but to work in the coal mines of South Wales – the government of the day not having been sufficiently far-sighted to realise that conscripting miners into the Forces meant that comparatively few were left to dig out the, at the time, ever-necessary coal! There, at Abercarn in the Western Valley of (then) Monmouthshire, I was billeted with a family of 'Born-again' Christians and regaled with accounts of various minor miracles, including phantasms of lambs seen to walk up aisles: miraculous cures and balls of light over the valleys presaging the Second Coming. Regrettably I personally witnessed none of these, having to be content with hearing various congregation members 'speaking in tongues' from time to time.

By 1950 I'd been married for a couple of years and my UFO interest was zero when the following incident occurred – at 2am on the morning of my daughter's first birthday, this later enabling me to pinpoint the date of the occurrence with accuracy

At the time my wife and I were living in an upstairs flat off Coldharbour Lane in Brixton, South London. The bedroom faced south: the windows were covered by moderately thick curtaining: our daughter lay asleep in a cot at the side of the bed.

An alarm clock with luminous dial atop the dressing table, together with the curtains, through which I could make out the vague shape of a full or near-full moon were all in my line of vision. After a couple of hours sleep I awoke. I was lying on my

Chapter 4 – JUST A FEW THOUGHTS
Norman Oliver

back, but, on attempting to turn over to a more comfortable position, found I was unable to move so much as the proverbial muscle: indeed not even the twitch of a muscle. My eyelids were the only movable body feature!

The length of time I was immobile seemed to me immense, but the clock confirmed it as being just under two minutes. That couple of minutes, though, seemed an age, an extended age, an age during which I attempted without success to move various parts of my body. Finally I managed to extract a single slight twitch from the upper segment of a little finger. From this point the power of movement gradually returned over my whole body. I turned over on my right side, noting as I did so that the hazy circle of the Moon was no longer to be seen through the curtaining – in my drowsy state attributing this to my changed position in the bed. Immediately I fell asleep, waking at the usual hour in the morning.

On recalling what had happened during the night, I discussed it with my wife, who was really of the opinion that I'd dreamt it anyway! Unusually, my daughter had not woken either of us at any time – normally she'd be pretty restless and as a consequence, so would we!

The incident was not repeated, but a few months later I came across a magazine item which referred to 'sleep paralysis', this being a condition where precisely the same symptoms I had evinced may be experienced. It would often recur, the article said, but in fifty subsequent years it has never recurred with me.

Some ten years after the incident, having moved to Lee Green in South London where the family remained for some 30 years I joined the British Astronomical Association. Later I was to become, as Larry, a Fellow of the Royal Astronomical Society. In the former capacity I was involved with satellite tracking and the thought came to me, "You're checking the movement of satellites, why not check out the position and phase of the Moon on the night of your 'paralysis'?" The phases of the Moon had not been uppermost in my thoughts at the time of my experience as it had been cloudy for some days prior to the occurrence. So – I checked out the position of the Moon on the first birthday of my daughter and, to my astonishment, found that it was 'New'.

Chapter 4 – JUST A FEW THOUGHTS
Norman Oliver

It was around the early 60s that I first became interested in UFOs, but then, UFO-wise, it was a very different world. Sighting reports; vehicle interference reports galore. Contact claims – commencing with Adamski – had been much reported for some years: even trips in spacecraft of one's own volition (recalling Daniel Fry's account of stepping into a remote-controlled craft for a trip over New York and back!). Abductions and 'Missing Time' experiences, though hadn't yet really appeared above the horizon.

Don't get me wrong: I'm not claiming to have been abducted, but, certainly in the climate of today, such an explanation for my nocturnal experience would be seized upon as being the most likely. However, no 'lost time' was apparently involved since I had – of necessity – been 'clock-watching' at the time! No, I don't believe that any 'involuntary displacement' of myself then occurred.

But – enough of that..........

Following an upsurge of UFO reports in the press, in the late 1960s I became, first, a member of the British UFO Research Association (BUFORA), then a Council Member, subsequently occupying a number of executive positions. In the 1970s I took over as its Journal Editor, in which capacity I became closely associated with Larry as he, at the time, was the National Investigations Co-ordinator for UFO reports and therefore able to supply me with up-to-date information on recent UFO occurrences.

Just before this, though, I was involved in an unusual incident whilst skywatching on the South Downs behind Worthing with Mark Stenhoff, now Head of Physics at a West London college. During the previous couple of years I had had several meetings with Philip Rodgers, a blind musician who claimed to have received a number of tape recorded messages from extra-terrestrials. I am not going into these here, but they were sufficiently interesting and inexplicable for us to take along a portable tape-recorder and switch it on for half-an-hour or so as an experiment during the course of the skywatch – well away from where we were sitting and certainly not anticipating any positive result. Nevertheless, we made a point of keeping very quiet whilst the recording took place and no-one else at all came by. The tape

Chapter 4 – JUST A FEW THOUGHTS
Norman Oliver

had been a new one brought along by Mark, still in its unopened packing.

On playing it back, it was absolutely soundless for some ten minutes, then, quite clearly came a male voice uttering the syllables *'Shub-shee'*, or so it sounded. I have since had it suggested to me by UFO researcher Jimmy Goddard that this might have been *'Sheo-sheoi'*, allegedly a 'Solex-Mal' phrase, said by George Hunt Williamson to mean *'To the apples we salt we return'*.

From around 1982 my UFO interest had, of necessity, to be curtailed due to family problems and I was only intermittently involved with the subject, though keeping abreast of events worldwide. I retired to the Lincoln area and, following the death of my first wife in 1991, went over to Thailand for a while and it was there that I met my second wife, Pom and her sisters, one of whom, Ratanaporn, I introduced to Larry as he has related elsewhere.

Some years later, we divorced and in 1998 I married for a third time, once again in Lincolnshire but now closer to the sea near the resort of Skegness and it was here that the 'Chimes' episode – dealt with fully in Chapter 12 occurred. Shortly after my return from Thailand however, there was one episode worthy of recounting, though I would strongly doubt a connection with any other occurrence. Such a connection could, at the most I would consider, be purely peripheral.

On a raw, cold, January day I had moved in to a third floor flat at Canwick Hall near Lincoln. Having managed to deposit my belongings I returned to the car and promptly slipped on a patch of ice with a resultant broken wrist. My car, which I had purchased a few months earlier, was consequently left to its own devices in the broad parking bay at the front of the Hall. With my right arm in plaster and a sling, about the best I could do was to keep it clean and run the engine once in a while.

It was on one such occasion I thought I'd test to see if I'd any strength to speak of in my right hand and, after cleaning the car, placed both hands on the bonnet, pressing down as hard as I could to see if I could move the car up and down on its springs at all. Well, maybe I managed a millimetre, maybe I didn't. It

Chapter 4 – JUST A FEW THOUGHTS
Norman Oliver

certainly wasn't prone to move at all for my left hand, let alone my right and stared at me as much as to say, "You'll have to do better than that!"

I gave it best and walked off. After about ten paces I looked back, when, to my amazement, there was my car bouncing up and down on its springs as if there was no tomorrow! There must have been between nine inches and a foot of up and down motion. No one else at all was around. I'd turned the engine off before locking the doors, but there it was, clearly enjoying dancing around all by itself with no apparent human involvement. I stood and watched. The 'bouncing' continued for at least two minutes, after which time I went back to it and attempted to get it to resume. Nothing I could do would make it budge the slightest!

A few days later, the manager of the flats said to me, *"The other day"* – a different day to my experience – *"The other day I was looking out of my window and I saw your car bouncing up and down on its springs – thought at first it must be children, but there were none around – in fact there was no one at all! Then I wondered if you were underneath it, but, especially considering your own right hand was 'out of action' this didn't seem to make much sense"*. I told him it had happened before, and subsequently, until my departure many months later, I felt he always viewed both me and the car with grave suspicion – I wasn't so sure about the car myself!

I was even less sure when, about six weeks later I was sufficiently recovered to drive and, on two or three occasions, after visiting a friend near Skegness, both headlights and sidelights cut out on dangerous bends on unlit country roads whilst driving after dark. On each occasion I'd managed to negotiate the bends and bring the car to a standstill, but it could well have been otherwise. I had the wiring checked but no fault could be found. However, immediately after the check my sidelights began behaving in an odd manner. First one would go out, then, as it came back on, the other would decide to black out and so on. On two occasions I took it to a garage but, on stopping there everything would be normal! One light would usually remain off if I was parked at the Hall, but should I take it in for a 'check-up' all would be operating normally.

Chapter 4 – JUST A FEW THOUGHTS
Norman Oliver

Some months later I got rid of the car, but I've always regretted I didn't get in touch with the previous owner to see if they'd experienced similar 'difficulties'. At a pinch I could have passed off the car's electrical eccentricities as wiring problems – despite garage assurances, but NOT when associated with its other gymnastics! I wonder about it to this day, and also as to whether its subsequent owner experienced similar 'auto-unaccountabilities'. Or was the car trying to tell me something??!!

As a prelude to the next chapter, which is solely concerned with ideas and suggestions about Larry's experiences, let me jot down a few of my own cosmological thoughts and ideas. Through the ever-changing background of my early life, whilst I had been brought up with Christian beliefs, these had varied in degree with the circumstances in which I found myself. So, whilst originally in a Baptist family, when evacuated as a schoolboy in the course of World War II I was then introduced to both Methodism and the C.of E. Come my coal-mining days, as aforesaid I was billeted with a fundamentalist family. A few years later, on marriage, after a close examination of various beliefs, I became a Catholic which, 'technically' I am to this day – but only technically!

My view of God was – and is – that, since He was supposed to be both omniscient and omnipotent, there was only one way this could be achieved, namely by actually BEING everywhere. 'God' had therefore to be a 'ray system' an 'energy system' – light is perhaps an appropriate analogy – Who/Which could be 'tapped into' in many different ways. Indeed, why should not everything, everybody which/who has ever existed be part of this 'energy system'?

In my innocence (or ignorance), on first arriving at this conclusion I considered my thoughts to be unique. However, amongst just a few diverse books and sources that consider such a proposition to be accurate are:-

SynchroDestiny,*(1) by Deepak Chopra: *The Wiccan Handbook,**(2) by Sheena Morgan: *The Handbook for the New Paradigm: Embracing the Rainbow* and *Becoming* *(3): The books and tapes on the subject of *Manifestation**(4) by Dr. Wayne W. Dyer and numerous other sources, not to mention, of course that

Chapter 4 – JUST A FEW THOUGHTS
Norman Oliver

this proposition forms directly or indirectly a basis of many Eastern religions.

Enough, though, of my own background. Let us proceed to my second chapter and some of the circumstances I feel need to be addressed concerning the 'Mi Experience' and to which I consider the foregoing paragraphs may well have relevance. Included also will be a few further thoughts and (I trust) pertinent points on the subject.

(1)Published 2003 by Harmony Books/Ebury Press,Random House, 20, Vauxhall Bridge Rd, London SW1V 2SA
(2)Published 2003 by Vega, 64, Brewery Road, London N7 9NT
(3)All available by phoning 1-800-729-4131 or e-mailing global@nohoax.com
(4)Tape/book lists from Nightingale Conant, 7300 North Lehigh Avenue, Niles, Illinois, USA.1-800-323-5552

Chapter 5 – "....AND A FEW MORE...."
Norman Oliver

First, to put my thoughts into, so to speak, chronological order and begin with one or two observations on Larry's teenage 'duplicate' in Bow. To me now, whilst the existence of Mi in our own spatial universe has to be considered, I lean more and more towards the possibility that 'his' home may not be in our own space at all, and either that he was from a different time frame or time-line altogether or from a parallel dimension. Larry was never able with absolute certainty to establish a frame of reference so far as his actual whereabouts was concerned and 'Time' was always high on the agenda between them. On a number of occasions, when relating his experiences, Larry has quoted my thoughts on various incidents via my e-mails. I don't believe that what I am now writing modifies them to any great degree, though some development of those thoughts plus a few new ones may well be in evidence

So – back to Bow Road. In this experience Larry first felt a 'slowing-up' a 'blurring', if you like, of Time as he crossed the second carriageway. Compare this feeling with that felt by many UFO/Alien experiencers. To give one or two examples:- my own postman buttonholed me one day and related an experience he and his wife had had some years back at their home in Skegness. It was November: they were looking out of their front window one dark evening when they saw an enormous delta shape appearing in their line of sight with 'myriads of sparkling lights' underneath barely more than a few hundred feet up. This huge object was moving at almost walking pace. They both said they experienced a 'coldness' and a feeling of 'Time slowing': of being 'suspended in Time and Place' for a few moments. Then, the object began to go out of sight over the rooftops. They went to the back of the house, but – there was nothing. The object had either zoomed off at tremendous speed or disappeared completely. As it came out of nowhere and similarly disappeared, is this not consistent with it materialising from and back into another Time or another Dimension?

Again, take the case of three women from Telford back in 1980. They were travelling by car when a huge circular craft came out of nowhere, hovering low above a nearby field. They subsequently found they had experienced time loss and, under

Chapter 5 – "....AND A FEW MORE...."
Norman Oliver

hypnotic regression, individually gave accounts of abduction into the craft. In their case, too, there had been a feeling, common to all, of being 'suspended in Time'; being in, so to speak, a 'nothingness'. Strangely, too, none of them had observed the craft taking off in a normal way. All they had were mental 'still' pictures of it being first almost on the ground, then about two or three hundred feet up and finally just a small circular object in the distant sky; its departure was, as it were, seen as three photographic 'stills', not as an object following a rising flight path into the sky. Again, quite possibly distortion of Time – or exiting and re-entering co-existent space rather than our own.

Finally, UFO-wise, there was the experience of a biker travelling to Doncaster on the A1 at night with a passenger in August 1982. A light approached from the west in a shallow glide. It stopped above the opposite side of the A1 and could just be seen as a very vague 'shape' with a white light and a red flashing light. By now the biker had pulled over onto the hard shoulder and he flashed his bike's headlight at the object. Immediately the light "seemed to explode in a maelstrom of light and motion" and shot across the road, hovering above him and his passenger at a height of under 100 feet. This object was 'huge' and emitted a very strong white light from a frontal hemispherical 'dome'. It also had flat, seemingly self-coloured panels of different colours. It was silent. Its appearance resembled "two vaguely cruciform shapes butted together at the 'meeting arms' of the crosses."

Traffic on the A1 was moving normally – no-one else seemed the slightest bit interested. The biker experienced 'a strange sense of isolation', became afraid and charged his bike back onto the road away from the scene and sped away southwards. After some days he decided to revisit the area, but could find no location that satisfied all the elements of his encounter. At no point could trees, telegraph poles, a farmhouse and so on be found together as they had been on the night of his experience. Does this again not suggest that other Time Lines or Dimensions may have been involved? This 'Oz factor' is present in many such experiences (# book reference).

I have digressed.

Chapter 5 – "....AND A FEW MORE...."
Norman Oliver

Let me again return to the point where Larry 'met himself' as a schoolboy. Might it not just be that two Time Lines /Two Parallel Dimensions coincided for Larry at this particular juncture? Maybe in the 'slowing up' Larry could even have appeared to his 'twin' – just as his 'twin' appeared to Larry once he had reached the further pavement. Also, as an aside, since the entity 'Mi' had two pupils in each eye I dubbed these as 'twin' pupils. Could there be an allegory or association of ideas here? Mi had 'twin pupils' – and on the pavements of Bow, what did we have at that point – twin 'pupils'!!

Moving on, I am attracted by the possibility of different dimensions coinciding for another reason. Might it just be that our 'dimension' and that of Mi only coincide at specific intervals? In that case, should 'Mi's Dimension' have precisely the same properties, then there could be a coincidence at specific, regular dates and times. However, should there be a difference in their properties, as, indeed has been put forward by Larry in other pages, then any temporal coincidence that occurred would presumably be irregular.

In particular two points interest me. Firstly, why did not Mi actually put in an appearance when the 'crying baby' was heard on the first occasion in Larry's home in Petts Wood? Secondly, was there a connection timewise, not just between these two occasions, but between THEM and Larry's schooldays experience? Let us have a look at the dates themselves:-

Larry was born on December 8th. 1942: his 'Bow' experience occurred when he was 13 years of age in May/June 1955, some six months after his birthday. The 'crying baby' was first heard in August 1976 – in England: this recurred in Thailand in January 2000. My first thought was that there might be a near correlation in the period between the 'Bow' incident and the baby crying in Petts Wood: also between that date and the crying heard in Thailand. However there is an actual gap of twenty-one years between the first and the second, whilst the period between the second and third is approximately twenty-three and a half years

There is also the thought, of course, that Time and Place did not matter: so far as Mi was concerned it could be an

Chapter 5 – "....AND A FEW MORE...."
Norman Oliver

irrelevance: indeed, it could even be possible that, to Mi, there was no time gap at all between the two occurrences. This might, for one thing, be how Mi managed to 'keep tabs' on Larry's movements over a period of more than twenty of our years – another point that has always had me wondering!

The suggestion too, that the dimensions of Mi and ourselves might touch at specific intervals might just also be relevant to the abrupt manner of Mi's 'disappearance'. Thinking 'sideways' to the last paragraph, the possibility has to be included that, if the two dimensions only 'touched' for a short while at specific intervals, then this also could be the reason, both for non-contact in the first instance and for its abrupt termination on the second occasion. It is possible too, that such a termination could automatically mean the termination of the recipient's knowledge of the 'information exchange' altogether and that the termination was not necessarily under Mi's control.

Be that as it may, let me return for a moment to the point of similarities in the length of gaps between occurrences. As I've just shown, whilst there may not have been a great difference timewise between them, there WAS a difference. However, that changes if, instead of taking the first 'crying' as a pivotal point, we look instead at the time when Larry 'saw his father's face' instead of seeing a plant pot and flowers. This incident happened on August 12th. 1978, almost exactly two years after the first 'baby's cry'. Here, there is practically a 'reverse' correlation and the first gap changes to twenty-three years and three months, whilst the second becomes twenty-one years and six months. However, to me it is not the 'gap' that is intriguing, but the date of the appearance of Larry's father – August 12th. Indeed, the first 'crying baby' incident was not far away from this date, being in the last two weeks of August 1976.

So – why am I intrigued by August 12th? Almost at the same time that Larry's 'Mi' experience unfolded at his Udornthani home I had just become interested in The Montauk Project and the Philadelphia Experiment*. Even to outline both of these would take up several chapters, but the gist, the flow of events alleged to have taken place was as follows:-

Chapter 5 – "....AND A FEW MORE...."
Norman Oliver

It is believed that, on August 12th. 1943, the USS Eldridge was involved in an 'invisibility' experiment at Philadelphia, USA. This was primarily to see if 'radar' invisibility could be obtained, but it apparently resulted not only in the ship becoming invisible to the human eye also, but in it being transported nearly one hundred miles and reappearing in Norfolk, Virginia. When again visible in Philadelphia, it was found that most of the crew had been affected mentally, whilst a number were dead, some having even been 'merged' into the structure of the ship.

Further allegations were made* that the Eldridge had also 'time-connected' with a base at Montauk, Long Island, New York State and that two of its crew were then the subject of Time-travel and Time-line experiments that were being made at this base. The actual date in Time the Eldridge was said to have connected with, was August 12th. 1983. To cut a long story short, scientists working at the Montauk base were said to have discovered that the Earth has a biorhythm peaking every year on August 12th., with maxima occurring every twenty years –1943, 1963, 1983, 2003 and so on and this formed a link for the U.S.S. Eldridge to travel in time. This biorhythm may well have both an occult and metaphysical connection.

As I mentioned earlier, my own interest in the Montauk affair commenced almost exactly at the same time as Larry's 'MI' experience. Hence my feeling that there is a strong 'Time' connection between the two. Hence also my interest in the fact that the date when Larry 'saw' his late father was August 12th. 1978. Also, of course, as with, for example, sunspots, it would be likely that, whilst the maximum of Earth's biorhythmic period would be August 12th, it would still be close to that maximum for a week or so on either side, hence the first 'crying baby' towards the end of August 1976 could well come into the equation also.

The other major connection with the Montauk events is that many of those taking part in the experiments there sustained, and still experience, both minor and major synchronicities in their lives. I found almost immediately that I too was experiencing the same, and Larry's accounts reveal very many coincidences and synchronicities – especially with numbers – the numbers 3 and 8

Chapter 5 – "....AND A FEW MORE...."
Norman Oliver

in particular. To give but one example that happened to me very soon after my Montauk interest developed. In April 2000 I was in Arkansas in the U.S.A and, having spoken at the UFO Conference in the town of Eureka Springs, I was invited down to stay near the town of Mena in the southern part of the State. The airfield there was one that had been the centre of allegations of presidential-associated drug-running in past years and my hosts took me on a tour both of the town and the airfield. When I returned to England I commenced e-mail communication with Peter Moon, the editor and co-author of several Montauk books.* I had not known him before, neither had he heard of me. My e-mail made no mention of my Arkansas trip. However, amongst other things, in his first e-mail back he asked me whether I knew that Mena had originally been a name and home for the Montauk Indians and that Mena airfield had been the centre of a drug ring. If one thinks of the number of towns and number of states in the U.S.A. plus the drugs connection, the odds against my even having heard of Mena must have been considerable, let alone my having stayed there and been taken round that particular airfield.

Before I leave Mi and have a look at later experiences, a few further thoughts. Was Mi in fact a sentient being, or was 'he' the figurehead, as it were, of someone who was? A celestial 'ventriloquist's dummy', if you like. Could he have been a 'representation' through which some other entity was communicating – an entity who wished their appearance not to be seen? I have always been struck by the fact that it was up to Larry to ask questions and Mi would answer or 'speak' about those – no information was ever volunteered, nor, to the best of my knowledge were any questions asked of Larry about anything connected with Earth. The sole reason for the meetings appeared to be to pass on information to Larry about subjects that he – Larry – raised, and only then if the questions were the 'right' ones. Nor, of course, does it follow that what Mi had to say was the 'last word' on the subject! Aliens – of any description or persuasion may be as equally at fault in their beliefs and interpretations of events as we are! Nevertheless, were I to have been in the same position as Larry with similar communications being received, I would

Chapter 5 – "....AND A FEW MORE...."
Norman Oliver

certainly have taken it that not only had the entity concerned, for some reason taken a good deal of trouble to get in personal touch with me, but that he must have had a very good reason for so doing.

Finally, so far as Mi is concerned, to quote Larry concerning his sessions with Mi. *"What seemed to have happened was that my 'encounter' reprogrammed all previous images* (from his meditation sessions*) and replaced them with just the one – Mi. When I ask a question and get an answer, there is no colour change. The image colour is green, but when I receive an answer, part of it changes colour, the whole slowly disappearing, allowing me to travel on further till I meet the changed image again...."* Also, on another occasion *".....It seems I can revisit answers when I restart a meditation, and always I seem to have to start at the beginning again. But I can only revisit a certain number of times since earlier answers have already been 'deleted'....."*. On reading this from Larry, I couldn't help thinking of a comparison with a computerised web site – where you 'explore' one particular facet of that site and then return to its home page.

Just two or three more thoughts before leaving the Mi part of Larry's experiences. *'Can everywhere to 24'*, Mi said, on being asked about his place of origin. Might that not just have meant, 'I can travel anywhere within the first twenty-four dimensions'? Or 'time-lines', or something similar? There is also, of course, the question as to numbers not being used in their systems. How and why, then, was a number used here? It would seem that Larry had to explain our own numerical system to the entity, so how come a number was volunteered before this? Also, if one postulates that another dimension is involved, would that dimension necessarily have, for example, the same stellar and other references, such as Mira, which form part of Larry's detailed mathematical and numerological investigations?

O.K., so let's now have a look at those experiences of Larry's which seemed unconnected with the entity at all – the 'blur', the 'disappearing ladies' and, in particular, the male voice associated with one of the latter, which said, *"It's there in front of you, three hundred years ago."*

Chapter 5 – "….AND A FEW MORE…."
Norman Oliver

Firstly, do these occurrences have anything to do with Mi? My own opinion would be, "No, not directly, but they could well have been occasioned by Larry being, so to speak, 'sensitized' by the encounters and becoming more susceptible, more sensitive to incursions or excursions by other entities, either from different dimensions or from another Time or Time Frame." I certainly feel here that 'Time' is once again part of the equation.

The 'blurs' could possibly be a 'side-effect' of interdimensional experience – again, a sort of 'sensitization' to entities 'not quite in focus' or becoming vaguely visible through a 'screen' lessened by that sensitization. The 'disappearing ladies' – I'm not quite so sure about those ladies in such a context – maybe they were, literally, time-travellers in our own spatial dimension. Think back for a moment to that final moment – well, final up to the time of writing this at any rate, where the male voice behind Larry repeated those words in the previous-but-one paragraph.

O.K. We have the 'lady' sitting down in front of him. On hearing the words, Larry turns, anticipating seeing a materialised male behind him. But – were the words directed at HIM? Might it not have been that, some three hundred years in our own future, 'time-vacationing', for example, could have become an alternative to a tropical holiday and that the male voice emanated from a futuristic 'Time-tour representative?' Fanciful, perhaps, but no more so, if one thinks about it than any other possibility.

"Now, having just been through the 23rd. and 22nd. centuries to see what the masses looked like and what they were doing, now, right in front of you, there is a typical specimen from the 21st." might well have been the full thrust of what the 'man' behind Larry was saying to the 'woman' in front of him! And the woman, or women on the other occasions could well have been having a 'free' day to 'have a look round at their leisure'!

There could be many other suggestions as to the whys and wherefores of Larry's 'Mi' experiences and those that subsequently occurred. Why not see what other possibilities *you* can come up with, taking into account Larry's detailed comparisons, numerological and mathematical deductions and all the synchronicities involved and uncovered?

Chapter 5 – "....AND A FEW MORE...."
Norman Oliver

#New BUFORA Journal No.6 February 2003. 'Experiences', Judy Jaafar

*The Montauk Project. Experiments in Time. Preston B.Nichols and Peter Moon ISBN 0-9631889-0-9

Montauk Revisited. Adventures in Synchronicity. Preston B.Nichols and Peter Moon. ISBN 0-9631889-1-7

Pyramids of Montauk. Explorations in Consciousness. Preston B.Nichols and Peter Moon. ISBN 0-9631889-2-5

All books available from SKY BOOKS, Box 769, Westbury, NY 11590-0104, U.S.A.

Part 2 – Chapter 6 – Chickened out

Introduction

In Part 1 I followed the sequence of events as closely as possible to dates in which the events occurred. In Part 2 I will only do so where it is necessary. There are three reasons for this.

1 At various times research was being carried out along several different lines connected to events that occurred at different times. Some results were not found to be valid until later on.

2 Secondly, there was computer malfunction as mentioned in the Preface.

3 This reason is even more incredible than that of the 'loss of memory'. Read on.

During early September 2000, Norman had a couple of things happen to him, though whether they are related to my experience is unknown. Below are Norman's own words written in two e-mails to me.

MC3etc

Thu, 7 Sep 2000

"Hi Larry,

Many thanks for your last e-mail. I may be a few days late in sending over further thoughts on Mi – and now I'm postponing these because of the following. It may well not have anything to do with Mi, though it did occur about a quarter of an hour after I'd finished re-reading MC3. I hope I can explain myself properly, but it would seem it could be said I had almost the opposite type of experience to your being 'disconnected', so to speak. As I say, it COULD be connected with Mi, but it could also be that I've been taking on – or thinking of taking on – too many possible 'avenues of activity' – projects such as short stories, a couple of books, lectures, Bufora activities and so on, apart from the perennial ones of the garden, decorating etc. etc. and I'm finding it difficult to keep them all going."

"Anyway:- Outside the front fence of the bungalow, there's a 6-foot overgrown strip that the Council's supposed to maintain – along with similar ones outside other bungalows/houses. They

Part 2 – Chapter 6 – Chickened out

don't, of course, do so! So – I've cleared it, painted the fence and put down about 50 large stones from a former rockery in the back garden, having painted them all red. (Looks quite effective and ties in nicely with the name 'Stepping Stones'!). However, three days ago I went out there – as I say, after re-reading MC3 – and clipped away at the remaining 'grass' to finish things off."

"This is extremely difficult to describe adequately – I tried it with Maisie and think I managed to do so up to a point. However, let us say that I have a number of different areas of thought that regularly surface at some point during the day. For example: Story writing and content: Talks/Lectures and content: UFOs: USA and friends there: Thailand and ditto: Star Trek: The Bungalow: Lincolnshire: Mi: Relatives: Holidays: Schooldays: London etc. etc. When I'd almost finished clipping I suddenly found I was thinking about any one of these or others, but my mind was immediately and uncontrollably passing on to another area where, however, incidents/people from my previous thoughts were included, then on again to another area, but including previous ones at the same time. This went on rapidly any number of times, like a dream where anything and everything is possible and logical. Sort of, say, Captain Picard turning up at my old school and laying turf at the bungalow – which was in the USA – that type of thing. As I say, perfectly logical in a dream, but not when one is awake and working at the time! Also, though I 'knew' that all this was perfectly logical – as it would have been were it a dream with 'x' numbers of subjects intertwined, at the same time I was also aware that in reality it was a load of nonsense. A dichotomy of thought outside uncontrolled thought, one might say. There were no other effects, visual or otherwise at the time, though I was 'drained' afterwards, this gradually rectifying itself over a couple of days, but I was in this 'waking dream' for about ten minutes and even after that for some time had to be careful how my thoughts were tending to move. As I say, all the 'steps' in this 'waking dream'(which I couldn't – as with most ordinary dreams – remember properly afterwards) seemed completely logical, though at the same time I was aware they were nonsense – incidents, possibly decades apart, crushed together, so to speak."

Part 2 – Chapter 6 – Chickened out

"Anyway, after about 10 minutes, I went indoors, realising that things were progressing faster and faster, and I didn't want to emulate the Oozelum bird and disappear you know where! Things then gradually settled down, but although getting back to normal, I found it was inadvisable to follow any particular line of thought very far without beginning to 'drift back' into this illogical 'waking dream' state.."

"Currently feel more or less back to normal, but am doing some minutes meditation morning and night in conjunction with mental exercises – concentrating on visualising colours: repeating 'master words': positive phrases etc. etc. I've even tried the Wicca 'ring of salt' routine – more just in case anyone's trying to 'get at me' rather than attributing demonic origin to Mi!!"

"Enough of that, though. Your Egyptian 'Goddess of the Sea'. I've gone through my 'GUIDE TO WORLD MYTHOLOGY' and, not just Egypt, – I can't find a woman in any of around 25 other mythologies who WAS: they're all male! The nearest reference I could get was to the Egyptian Goddess ASTARTE in connection with the God SETH."

"SETH was apparently given two 'foreign' wives by the other gods to compensate him for ceding the right to the throne to HORUS. These wives were ANAT and ASTARTE. The latter was a daughter of a Sun God PTAH and it says she was commonly depicted as a naked woman carrying weapons, often shown on a horse – which doesn't exactly tie in!! However, the following quote from the book might just have some relevance...– Seth's other foreign wife, ASTARTE, appears in a myth in which the Gods of Egypt are in conflict with a Sea God. PTAH and the ENNEAD were forced to pay tribute to the Sea. The 'Harvest Goddess' RENENTUTET carried their tribute of Gold, Silver and Lapis Lazuli to the shore, but the insatiable Sea wanted more, and threatened to enslave the Gods of Egypt if he did not receive it. RENENTUTET sent a bird as a messenger to ASTARTE's house to tell her to take tribute to the Sea. ASTARTE wept when she heard this. She took the tribute to the shore, but on reaching her destination she sang and mocked the Sea. Then the Sea demanded ASTARTE herself. The beautiful Goddess appeared before the

Part 2 – Chapter 6 – Chickened out

ENNEAD, who gave her a dowry of jewels, including the necklace of NUT and the signet ring of GEB. ASTARTE went down to the shore carrying the treasure, but Seth went with her to fight the Sea. The end of the story is missing, but it is most likely that the strength of SETH overcame the Sea and that ASTARTE was saved. –"

"Have gone through the book's illustrations to see if I can come up with any deity conforming to your description of dress etc., but no success so far – will keep on trying. As a thought, there might be a clue or two in one of W.Raymond Drake's books, or, come to think of it, in an article or two of his that he sent me. I'll see what turns up – if anything – by the time I next e-mail."

"Reckon that's about it for the moment. All best wishes to you both.

Yours Norman"

14 Sep 2000 11:
Me, Mi and the Pumps

"Hi Larry,
Many thanks for your e-mail of 8th. September. Can't say I'm feeling quite 100% yet, but am getting there and have had no actual recurrence of my 'mental maelstrom'. Found your comments and suggestions very helpful: I ceased using the 'colour concentration' after reading them just in case, but what I'd been doing in this direction was mentally to visualise the spectrum colours for about 10 seconds or so in turn, so it wasn't quite as though I was concentrating on 'my' colour – but I have to admit I was beginning to have a partiality for green. Appreciated also your thoughts on 'mental doors', which I found very useful. Have also been meditating in conjunction with 'Master Words' of the 'Tranquil' and 'Relaxing' variety. Think you may well be right also that Mi could have been 'cashing in' on a touch of the 'mental overloads'. Anyway, so far, things are progressing satisfactorily. Have been reducing my 'workload' and also its variety so that I concentrate on one thing at a time. Currently am making quite a good job (I think!) of converting half of the back garden into a

vegetable garden and removing the former rockery there – plus a fair bit of re-turfing. Think that's about all for now.
*   All the very best to you both. Yours Norman.*"

The following paragraphs give a brief idea of the avenues considered.

Fri, 26 Jan 2001. Mi, Loki and Giants

"*Hi Larry. First of all, let me give you a few details of what I've come across in Norse Mythology; Something just might be relevant here, but I'm not at all sure exactly what. I've only 'scratched the surface' reference-wise so far and will look at in more detail before I send again. Anyway, briefly:- 'Scandinavian Deities of the Viking Age' as follows:- Balder, son of Odin, doomed to die. Freyja, goddess of fertility, sister of Freyr. Freyr, god of fertility and royal ancestors Frigg, queen of heaven and wife of Odin. Heimdall, watcher over Asgard, and known as father of mankind. Hoenir, a silent god, companion of Odin. Loki, a trickster companion of the gods. Njord, god of sea and ships, father of Freya and Freyr. Odin, god of magic, inspiration, battle and the dead, and ruler of the gods. Thor, god of sky and thunder, protector of law and the community. Tyr, remembered as the binder of the wolf Ull, god with skis and bow, worshipped in Scandinavia.*"
    "*For some reason I feel that Loki might have some relevance. May be just because I saw the film 'The Mask', which featured Loki. However, quoting from my reference book regarding Ragnarok (which, as you rightly say, more or less equates with Armageddon).................. 'Loki, having broken free from his bonds, led the giants against the gods in the last great battle, known as Ragnarok. The world was under constant threat from the giants, who coveted the gods' treasures and the goddess Freyja, and threatened a return to chaos and sterility. Odin collected the greatest heroes who had fallen in battle in Valhalla so that they would support the gods. Thor wielded his hammer against the giants and kept them out of Asgard until Ragnarok'.*

Part 2 – Chapter 6 – Chickened out

Now look at the following 'introductory paragraph' to Balder, son of Odin:- 'Many of Odin's journeys were motivated by his wish to obtain knowledge of the future. He consulted runes, and also the head of the wise giant MIMIR (my capitals!!!), killed by the Aesir. He made dangerous trips to see other giants famed for their wisdom, and even called up the dead to question them. From them, he knew that he was doomed to be devoured by the wolf Fenrir, and that Loki was constantly plotting against the gods'."

"As I say, Larry, will have a good look at Norse mythology over the next few days and in particular, find out anything I can about the Giant MiMir – there's even a double 'Mi' here."

Date: Mon, 29 Jan 2001
"Hello, Larry,

Many thanks for yesterday's e-mail. I can't find any reference to Loki having been a court jester or entertainer at any time, but then I don't think either of the reference books I was looking through referred to his early life. I'll keep looking, both for him and court jesters (if any) elsewhere in other mythologies."

Even the question of Chickens was investigated, because domestic fowl originated in the forest areas which are now Eastern Thailand and Cambodia. I lived in Orpington which is the home of the Orpington Buff. Counting chickens however, seemed to be a wild goose chase, so this line of research was not continued, as it appeared to lead nowhere.

Chapter 7 – New beginnings

By November 2000 a lot of material had been accumulated, and it became clear that some kind of order was required to make any sense, if indeed there was any sense at all. Once we started to do this, so the 'coincidences' began to build up.

Having put many of my notes on to floppy disc, I placed most of my 'scribblings' in a folder and put them away in a safe place out at the back of the bungalow, a place where I frequently kept records of Tae-kwon-do etc. One day, while sorting out clothes that had been brought from England, I came across some long-sleeve shirts I had not worn for a long time. Then I picked up one of my favorites, which had a single chest design not unlike that of the clef symbol used in music, only it was facing in the reverse direction. A strange chill hit me and I started to think about the notes that had just been stored away.

Though the shirt design is not close to the clef shape the important point is that it reminded me of the drawing. This started a completely new search, and a more successful one.

In the original drawing I was thinking of a fetus, but I was now comparing this to the musical clef. Just by 'coincidence' the word 'Mi' happens to be the *third* in the Tonic Sol-fa, Doh, Ray, Mi. 'Mi' according to my large two volume Oxford English dictionary (1964), can be spelt with either an 'e' or an 'i', though 'Mi' appears to be the earlier version. It comes from the Latin word 'mira' (meaning 'wonderful'). This meant more to me than just a musical scale. It is the name of the only star that has a name in the constellation of Cetus. The common name is Mira Ceti, and the official name is Omicron Ceti.

However, this star was not named for any musical association, but for its Latin meaning – 'wonderful to look at': the original observer named the star 'wonderful star'. Even in the numbered name 'omicron' there is a 'mi' syllable. The term 'omicron' is taken from the Greek alphabet, and is the 15th letter, thus meaning object number 15 in the constellation.

So the Latin word 'mira' has two root meanings. It lends itself to musical associations and it was also used as part of the later word 'mirror'. Of course, one would use 'mira' to check one's look in the mirror. In the mirror one sees a 'mirror image', and this

Chapter 7 – New beginnings

becomes important later. One also might note that the original drawing is facing the opposite direction to a musical clef. A 'Mirror Image' perhaps?

So, suddenly things are changing – just because of the coincidental associations of the name Mi and the drawings.

Norman pointed out also the song from the film 'The sound of Music'.

'Doh, a deer, a female deer, Ray a drop of golden Sun, Me a name I call myself....' So 'Mi' is the third note. This reminds me of the sequences of threes. In case you had not already guessed it, Earth is the *third* planet from the Sun.

We had already seen the *three* most important dates in my life: my birthday on the 8th: my first marriage on the 8th. (I had *three* children. It was the third youngest child who was responsible for me getting out of my seat to check her when I heard the 'crying'). My departure from England on the 8th for Thailand, where Mi made contact.

Then there is the number 23. Ah, you might say, there are only two of those. The birth dates of your Mother and your *third* wife. Well, the other way about my birthday was referred to earlier. I have already mentioned that from the 8th of December there are 23 days to the last day of the year.

Three times eight equals twenty-four, and three times twenty-three equals sixty-nine. The number 69 will appear again. The number 8 is not exactly devisable by 3 and the same goes for 23, while the additions of the three occurrences are. So already there seems to be a series of threes'. Could it be there that there is a message here that the number 3 is important?

While Norman found several reference to 'gods' containing the syllable 'mi'(such as the MiMi associated with the Aborigines of Australia) perhaps the one associated with Odin was most worth considering. Mimir was associated with water, and Odin often consulted Mimir. The constellation Cetus is also associated with water. In ancient mythology Cetus was a sea monster sent by Neptune to kill Andromeda. Perseus killed the monster.

(Continued on page 61)

Chapter 7 – New beginnings

This is scanned copy of the copy of the drawing that I made during meditation sessions that I sent to Norman. In the upper left-hand corner, are the words 'embryo', 'baby' and 'womb', which indicates the way I was thinking. The outer circular enclosure remains undefined. The copy of the shirt design can be seen showing through with a slightly more bluish tinge.

Chapter 7 – New beginnings

Below, on the left, is the scanned copy of the shirt design, which I still possess today. Examples of clefs used in music writing are on the right.

clefs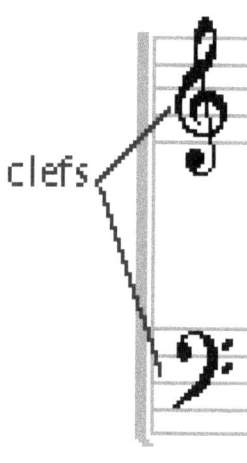

Chapter 7 – New beginnings

We were now in February 2001 and there was still a need to put all the information and the coincidences in some order. Indeed there were items that would need to be removed.

Basically there were three sections, the Mi experience itself, the concentrated dreams that came afterwards and the 'mysterious lady' appearances.

Unless there was some indication that the 'mysterious lady' was part of the experience it would be best to lay this section to one side. Indeed, Norman had pointed out to me that the Mi experience may have stimulated some part of my mind so as to make me more sensitive to other things.

We then looked at the mythological aspects and the idea of a 'trickster' came up a few times. The plausible thought that Thailand and my home in Orpington, prior to travelling to Thailand, linked by Fowl was, perhaps, a temptation to call it a link. Chickens are, however, well known for their contradictory nature, and have sometimes been used as a sign of bravery, while on the other hand, 'who is going to chicken out?' is well known. Thus I considered this part a possible ruse – 'a wild goose chase' – maybe to put us off course. This too, was put to one side

Considering the Tonic Sol-fa, a coincidence here is that notes are arranged in Octaves, or '8's'. It is vibrations that cause the sounds, which brings us into the study of Harmonics in Physics. There are also forms of Mathematical Progressions, known as Harmonics.

There is yet a third set. The Law of Octaves was introduced into Chemistry to explain periodical similarities between the Chemical elements known at that time. This Law is no longer used, but it led to the discovery in the late nineteenth century of what is now known in Chemistry as the Periodic Table.

Thus we have, coincidentally, another *three*, Physics, Mathematics and Chemistry, our three fundamental sciences upon which all the others are built.

There was yet another series of eight actually made up by series of three that were important in my life.

The patterns of Tae-kwon-Do are based on the philosophy of the 8 Trigrams from the Chinese I (pronounced 'ee') Ching, and

Chapter 7 – New beginnings

each Trigram is made up of 3 lines. They are listed below. Yet another '24'

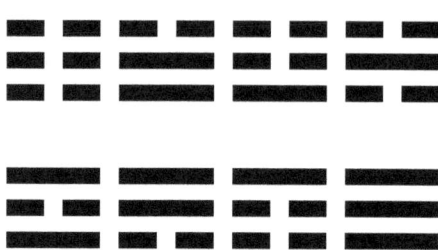

The shorter double lines are considered as broken lines. Combinations of these make up the 64 characters of the I Ching.

Just by coincidence, Norman and I, with the aid of 'askjeeves.com' found only one place in the world that had the single name of 'Mi' and that was in S.E. China. However, most maps do not show this town and its apparent location coincides with a town called Chang Sha, which has ancient origins. It seems that Chang Sha has long been an important transportation point. The map does not explain why the area shown on the Website translates the Chinese area as 'Mi', but it does so happen that one of the most important food transports is rice. There are several Chinese words with the Romanization of 'Mi', perhaps the most common one meaning 'rice'. Other meanings range from 'honey' to implications of divine processes. The 'i' in Chinese has two sounds, but when it comes after an 'M' sound the 'i' is pronounced as 'ee'.

We then began to wonder if this fitted in with any other research, and if so, how?

Meanwhile, I was also working with certain mathematical formulae and One line of approach was Harmonic Progressions. This basically involves taking a certain base number and dividing it by other numbers of regular increments, say 1,2,3 etc. and then adding the total. So I tried the simplest of all, with '8' and '3':

With a result of 27.24, as with the number 24, I was thinking in terms of some kind of period, but the only one that was found close to this was that of the Moon's sidereal revolution of

Chapter 7 – New beginnings

27.23 days. Then, considering the Moon, we have another coincidental '8', the main named eight phases of the Moon – Crescent, First Quarter, Gibbous, Full, Gibbous, Last Quarter, Crescent and New Moon; it must be pointed out however, that other 'sub-phases' are seen throughout the month. Although other planets in the Solar system affect the Earth, the Moon does so more noticeably because it is closer. The Moon is of major importance of course, in considerations that involve the Earth's Oceans. The other major effect from the Solar System is that of the Sun. The Sun and the Moon are both very important to us Human Beings in a physical sense and for calculating time periods. Thus, along with the Earth we have another set of three.

However, no figures yet obtained seem to involve the Sun. If the Moon was involved how could we confirm this?

One morning while I shaving and thinking about the other wrinkled face looking back at me, a thought struck me. Thinking of the 'mirror image' in Mi's answer to my questions, and the 'mira' meaning, perhaps there was a message here. What if I used the Earth as the original, showing Mi in China as being in the S.E quadrant? Where might this coincide on the Moon? Out came my Astronomical Atlas, and turning to the atlas of the Moon, S.W. quadrant. I first noted the well-known crater named Tycho, and further west was 'Wilhelm' but a little further westward, to my surprise, was a feature called 'Mee'.

So now the coincidences were building up to a point where by using a very small range of figures and words, there seemed to be links with the word 'Mi'.

Just when I thought a pattern was beginning to emerge, things took a turn for the worse.

The contents of my original scribblings and notes had been put on to floppy disc and the originals kept in a safe place, one that I used for Tae-kwon-do records. Looking for one of my floppy discs, wanting to refer to some notes, I could not find it. I kept all these discs in sections depending on whether they were notes, copies of letters etc. Mi references were all in one floppy disc file. However, the one marked 'Mi exp. notes' was missing. That was not all. There was a bonfire on a small piece of waste ground just

Chapter 7 – New beginnings

outside where I live. The family opposite usually starts a fire and people add their waste paper to this. There seemed to be something on it that I recognized – a blue folder. I rushed out to investigate, but whatever it was had now been burnt. On checking my 'safe place', the folder with my Mi notes was missing. There was no one else in the bungalow at the time but me. I simply could not believe this and later on I turned the bungalow inside out, but the file and the disc were not, and have not, been found. The only possible explanation is that I put the file on the bonfire myself. Talking to the old lady across the way, whose bonfire it was – and as she was close to it when I noticed it – I asked if she had seen anyone from my bungalow put something on the fire. She answered in the negative. If I had done so would she not have said that she saw me do so?

Loss of memory concerning the experience is one thing that may be acceptable, but missing the actual physical items having connection to the memory loss really does take a lot believing.

As if this was not enough, my computer and some discs became infected with Ethan and Astia Viruses and many other files were lost this way.

Norman passed on several alternatives to me as to what might have happened to the files including ideas that might have involved Mi. It seems now that we will never know the truth.

However, all new notes and researches (apart from those affected by the viruses) were still at hand, though perhaps a little disorganized. After getting over the disbelief of the missing material, it was back to study.

During late February Norman made a mistake when writing an e-mail to me, and he passed the comment that *I* might be twinned with Mi. Other points mentioned about Mi were that maybe Mi might have had an accomplice since there seemed to be a 'language problem' ('…can everywhere to twenty four…' for example). Also, according to surviving, un-filed notes, I appeared to have got the impression that Mi did not want to give any idea about Mi life gender.

By the middle of March 2001 research was progressing so much Norman decided to make it the subject of his American

Chapter 7 – New beginnings

Conference Lecture. One coincidence after another occurred, and by now I could no longer think of them as coincidences, because I had the strong feeling that we were on the right track. In the next chapter you will read the results of many hours' and many months' study, not to mention the continued large volume of communication between us both.

Chapter 8 – What's in a name?

Numbered letter matrix / name comparisons – refer to page 69

8 × 3

abc	def	ghi	jkl
mno	pqr	stu	vwx

Mira = 1331	Dale = 1132	Mi = 13	ra = 31
Time = 2312	Odin = 3132	Mars = 1131	Loki = 3323
Gods = 1311	Thor = 2233	trio = 2333	Moon = 1332
1131 = 6	1132 = 7	1311 = 6	1331 = 8
1332 = 9	2312 = 8	2333 = 11	3132 = 9
3323 = 11	3332 = 11		

6 × 4

a b c d	e f g h	i j k l	m n o p	q r s t	u v w x
Mira	1121	5	Moon	1332	9
Odin	3412	10	Time	4111	7
Loki	4331	11	Dale	4141	10
Thor	4432	13	trio	4213	9

3 × 8

a b c d e f g h	i j k l m n o p	q r s t u v w x			
Mira	5121	9	Moon	5776	25
Odin	7416	18	Time	4155	15
Loki	4731	15	Dale	4145	14
Thor	4872	21			
trio	4217	14			

Chapter 8 – What's in a name?

Numbered letter matrix / name comparisons – refer to page 69

4 × 6

a b c d e f g h i j k l m n o p q r s t u v w x

Mira	1361	11	Time	2315	11
Odin	3432	12	Moon	1332	9
Loki	6353	17	Dale	4165	16
Thor	2236	13	trio	2633	14

	8 × 3	6 × 4	3 × 8	4 × 6
Mira	1131	1121	5121	1361
Odin	3132	3412	7416	3432
Loki	3323	4331	4731	6353
Thor	2233	4432	4872	2236
Time	2312	4111	4155	2315
Moon	1332	1332	5776	1332
Dale	1132	4141	4145	4165
trio	2333	4213	4217	2633

[Note that in the 8×3 matrix the count for 'Mi' is the mirror image of the count for 'ra']

Chapter 8 – What's in a name?

Mi lives 'everywhere to 24'. We took the usual routes, looking at time of rotations, periods and so forth. However, 24 may satisfy other situations, one or all of which may play a part. For example, up to 24 hours may sound a little baffling but then, the term Right Ascension in Astronomy uses a 24 hour system, where 1 hour is equivalent to 15 degrees. The other point is that we must review the interpretation of '...up to 24'. For example, if I said to you that I had visited every house in a particular street up to number 24, what would you think? You could think there might be higher numbered houses in the street that I had not yet visited.

Using the same idea I thought about what is familiar to us that goes up to and beyond number 24. The obvious thing that came to mind was the English Alphabet, having 26 letters. If we number them as usual from A to Z, the letter X is number 24. The first thing that might be thought of is that X, Y and Z are the three letters commonly used to refer the X, Y and Z axes when drawing or referring to things in 3 dimensions. The number 26 is not wholly divisible by 3 whereas the number 24, IS.

Maybe Mi was trying to give us a clue by saying that the Mi dimension (or dimensions) only included what we usually refer to as the X axes and that Y and Z were to be excluded. This might mean that **we** could only see the Mi environment as a single line. Mi might possess other dimensions that we can't see.

How do we interpret A to W? It might mean that the letters, or numbers relating to them, have to be manipulated to provide the answer. If Mi had provided the clues then surely Mi would have done so in a way that I could understand. (Either that or Mi was going to have to upgrade my brain.)

The first attempt to look for possible connections was with some of the names that were involved, or were thought to be important. Linking this to the idea of 24 this would only take us up to the letter 'x' in the alphabet. So words containing 'z' or 'y' were excluded. Then, a Matrix type Code system, involving '8' and '3', and numbering each letter according to how many letters were in each set, was used.

On the next page is an example of the $8 \times (1 \times 3)$ Matrix system.

Chapter 8 – What's in a name?

[a b c] [d e f] [g h i] [j k l] [m n o] [p q r] [s t u] [v w x] and numbering all as [1 2 3].

Since Mira was a four-letter word, only four letter words were examined. For example:-

Mira equated to 1331, Dale = 1132, Moon = 1332.

The numbers were then added together sequentially. Mira = 1331 = 8

The complete list is on pages 66 and 67.

Mira is mentioned specifically here because immediately it can be seen that the number is made up of a 'mirror image' (mentioned earlier), '13' and '31' and the resulting addition is 8. Multiplying 1331 by 3 = 3993 will give the resulting sequential addition of 24. And just by *another* coincidence Ceti = 3223, which is another mirror image number. Adding the two together gives 4554, a <u>third</u> mirror image. So, at the very first outset of a simple system that I knew of, we can derive two numbers that are associated with one of the definitions of the word 'mira', and we derive an '8' along with the number mentioned by Mi – 24.

One strange feature is that the Moon is 1332 in three of the sets. The last 'sheet' is a list of all the figures contained in the 4 matrices. Again, looking at the figures for Moon, if 5776 is added sequentially we get 25, which also happens to be the sequential figure for the word count (see below) Earth, 52 and 25. You will notice that the two figures for Earth are mirror images. By adding the *three* sequential values for Moon we have $3 \times 9 = 27$. This number is as close as we can get in this system to the Moon's Sidereal period of revolution.

Obviously the Earth and the Moon have a connection, but we hardly expected to find it here. In the Thai section there is yet another connection.

We then decided to change our method. Names were given a total according to numbered letters of the alphabet. Two types of addition processes were considered. A straightforward name or word count, 'Arithmetic addition', and a sequential letter count, 'Seq. add.'. For example, the arithmetic count for Mira is 13 plus 9 plus 18 plus 1 = 41, and a sequential count of 13 = 4, 9 = 9, 18 = 9, 1 = 1 giving total of 23 as a sequential count. Ceti is 3+5+20+9

= 37 and 18. Note that the sequential are coincidental because 23+18 = 41.

When trying to interpret the dreams involving Norse Mythology I formed a sentence out of the names Loki, Odin and Thor, which was 'look hind trio'. This seemed a clumsy way to give a message about the three deities but on the other hand, maybe the word might be referring to another trio. Why did we continue to meet the number '3'? In the 1×3 section the numbers of Loki, Odin and Thor are 9, 10 and 11 which seemed interesting. The average of these is Odin, and the total sum would be 30, which again seems to indicate that '3' is important.

The complete list

	Arithmetic. Add.	Seq. add.	2nd Seq.
Ceti 3 5 20 9	37	19	10
Gods 7 15 4 19	45	27	9
Loki 12 15 11 9	47	20	2
Mars 13 1 18 19	51	24	6
Mira 13 9 18 1	41	23	5
Moon 13 15 15 14	57	21	3
Odin 15 4 9 14	42	24	6
Time 20 9 13 5	47	20	2
Thor 20 8 15 18	61	25	7
Cetus 3 5 20 21 19	68	23 (5 letter word)	

However, this method was not going to supply information about other names because they were longer than four letters.

We then decided to study a more complete list of names that did not involve the Matrix method, but included those names that were involved in the experience and those that seemed to be important from the dreams.

Now, I have a signature that uses just my first Christian name and my surname, Lawrence Dale. I only use my middle name, William, when necessary. Lawrence Dale = 81+22 = 103. The first thing that is noticeable is that the count for Dale is the

Chapter 8 – What's in a name?

same as the count for 'Mi'. I realize that there are many 'Dales' and the number 22 would be contained in all of them. However, Mi contacted one of them, so we must assume that the coincidence of both Mi and Dale is relevant. However, just as the word 'mira' had previously switched my thoughts to the star Mira, so did the word count for the everyday usage of my name, 103. 103 is the Atomic Number of the Chemical element that was given the name of...Lawrencium (*an Atomic number is the number of Electrons, or Protons, in one atom of the element*). This can be checked in any textbook on Physical Chemistry.

Lawrencium is a radioactive artificially made element with isotopes, the most stable one being isotope 260, with a 'half life' of about three minutes. It was produced at the Lawrence Berkeley Laboratories in America in 1961, hence the name. One point to mention here is that Lawrencium is a member of the Actinide series, all of which end their radioactive lives as Lead 207. I wonder, does Lead = Dale? The name count for Lawrencium is 119 with a sequential count of 47.

What becomes interesting here is that we have an object from the subject of Astronomy that is identified by one specific name and another that identifies its position. Then we have an object from another field, Chemistry, which also has a specific name and another number that identifies its position relative to all the other chemical elements. Mira, in the constellation Cetus, and Lawrencium, the 103rd element in the Periodic Table (*Hydrogen, the first element has an atomic number of 1*). Now, Mira Ceti has a total count of $41+23+37+18 = 119$ which equals the count for Lawrencium. What a coincidence!

One realizes that in the totality of the English Language there must be a great many 'coincidences' and a skeptic might suggest that is all we have here – coincidences. However, I would argue that we are dealing with a small and specific portion, related to a specific experience. So I therefore consider deductions here as being related to the experience. Indeed for what is yet to come, it would seem that we were somehow expected, or influenced, to tread these paths.

Using the same procedure as in the previous pages:

Chapter 8 – What's in a name?

	Arith. add –	Seq. –	2nd Seq
Carr 3 1 18 18	40	22	4
Cat 3 1 20	24	6	6
Dale 4 1 12 5	22	13	4
Dorothy 4 15 18 15 20 8 25	105	42	6
Elizabeth 5 12 9 261 2 20 8	88	43	7
Ellen 5 12 12 5 14	48	21	3
Huntington 8 21 14 20 9 14 7 20 15 14	142	52	7
Knoweldon 11 14 15 23 5 12 4 15 14	113	41	5
Lawrence 12 1 23 18 5 14 3 5	81	36	9
Lawrencium 12 1 23 18 5 14 3 9 21 13	119	47	11 =2
Norman 14 15 18 13 1 14	75	30	3
Oliver 15 12 9 22 5 18	81	36	9
Omicron 15 13 9 3 18 15 14	87	42	6
Pellis 16 5 12 12 9 19	73	37	10 =1
Simon 19 9 13 15 14	70	34	7
Thailand 20 8 1 9 12 1 14 4	69	33	6
Thomas 20 8 15 13 1 19	76	31	4
William 23 9 12 12 9 1 13	79	34	7

I had done my best to keep the two number systems as separate as possible but to be honest, some crossing of the systems seemed obvious and some deductions were made from this procedure. However, I have not intentionally 'cheated', because this would get us nowhere, and in the totality would be nothing but a skeptic's dream in tearing it apart. However, *more important* was that if Mi had really meant the experience to mean something, surely Mi (or any other intelligent life for that matter) would do things with such cross-references. That is to say, if one goes about it one way, it leads to certain results, and doing it the other way leads to a similar conclusion. If such an idea existed, I wanted to use the two systems so that they MIGHT verify each other. As you read on, in fact, this is exactly what has happened, and I must admit that some of my deductions came as a complete surprise, especially items of a personal nature.

Chapter 8 – What's in a name?

In the study a total of 30 words are used, of which 25 are nouns. The names used are only those that were experienced, or that we had discussed in a definite manner during our 'researches'. Indeed, we have not used any terms that <u>might</u> have possible links such words as 'Space', 'Astronomy' etc.

Thus, hopefully, any misuse of information has been avoided. There are words that have been deduced (Lawrencium for example), but they have not been introduced as a matter of convenience. It must also be remembered that Norman was instrumental in me arriving in Thailand, so it would seem that, added to the coincidences of previous chapters, Norman was definitely involved also.

The first result to note is that of Mira, the first two letters of which are Mi = 22. This we met earlier and Mira's constellation name, Omicron Ceti, will be discussed later.

The next result to be seen is that the number 23 in the sequential column occurs twice, Mira and Cetus. No other '23's' occur elsewhere (except with the birthdays on page 9) so we might deduce here that Mira and Cetus are not only connected in astronomical classifications, but these two are also connected in word counts. It is strange that the only named star in the constellation Cetus is Mira[†]. Thus, it would seem that the name Mira is where it **should** be for the purposes of 'someone'.

We can also notice here that there is a link between this section and the previous section with the matrix formation. The sequential addition for Mira Ceti was 13313223 = 18. Add this to the 23 from Mira's sequential count, 18+23 = 'Mira'. If we continue to add sequentially we have 9+5, which equals 14, a mirror image of 41.

We have already met the importance of the number 23 in a previous chapter. Was this meant to lead us into the deduction that Mira and Cetus were equally important? And was there another '23' that could be derived from the existing material to give another set of three? The answer is yes there is, and it is derived from yet another set of three. The addition of the sequential columns for Odin, Loki and Thor gives an average of 23. So from a set of three names we derive yet another 23. We now have six 23's.

Chapter 8 – What's in a name?

Was this an indication that we should transform our '3' into '6? Also in the sequential column, there seems to be the beginning of a possible sequence, from 20-29, but there are some gaps. So using existing material I decided to check to see if suitable derived names might exist.

Moon and Mira are 21 and 23 so Mi might fit as the 22 but other four-letter words might also fit, 'Star' for example from 'Time' and 'Mars'. Using Time and Odin we get 'Mind' and though it is true to say that Mi contacted me through my Mind, I am unsure if this fits anything else. On the other hand, Star would seem to fit because of Mira being a star. Mars had come up several times previously, and it is Odin and Mars that give rise to the name 'Tuesday'.

Having found the 'Mee' area on the Moon previously by using the mirror effect from Mi in China, the word count for Mee is 23 and 14, 14 being a mirror image of 41. So here is a possible cross-reference in the additions with Mee and Mira. This we have to hold in abeyance since this 23 is not from the sequential figures. Nonetheless, it is there and we can't simply ignore it because it doesn't fit in with the idea of a system of '3's'. What we may be looking at is the three separate 23's from the dates, three separate 23's from the sequential figures, and one that might be included in a comparative sense.

However another very important feature turns up. We can also deduce the word counts for Lawrence Dale, 103, and Norman Oliver from Lawrencium and (Mira) Ceti using the two values of Lawrencium, 103 and the word count 119; 119 + 37 = 156 which just happens to be the word count for Norman Oliver. So both first and last names are contained within the expressions for Mira Ceti and Lawrencium.

The conclusion at this point is that there is a connection between all these and that Mi may have used Lawrencium and Mira Ceti to make a link between me and Norman. Thus it would seem that Lawrencium and Mira Ceti are the focal points, and in the next chapter this seems to be confirmed. Other sequential addition possibilities were considered such as Thor plus Odin, Trio plus Mira and Elizabeth Dale + Lawrencium.*

Chapter 8 – What's in a name?

The word Cat has been is on the list since our pet cats, mentioned in an earlier chapter, were involved in a coincidence.

What is interesting here is that the results for Cat and Norman Oliver are divisible by 3. This is not the case for Lawrence Dale. So it would seem that Norman's link with Cat is stronger than that of mine. It may be noted here that in the cultures of China and Thailand it is still **actively** believed cats are special. If one is identified with certain properties of a Cat then you are being given a compliment.

Having found a link with Mira Ceti and Lawrencium, Mi might also have found a connection between Omicron Ceti and Lawrencium. This too eluded me for a while because using the same process as before Omicron Ceti has a count of 124.*

Now, subtracting the count for Omicron Ceti from the total count for Lawrencium equals 98 which at first sight appears to be an inert number as far we are concerned.* However, remembering Chemistry and again the Periodic Table, 98 is the Atomic number of Californium. This was one of the chemical elements from which Lawrencium was produced. The other chemical element used was Boron, which has an atomic number of 5. Though it may be a 'minor' connection, Boron connects to Mira – 'Californium' plus 'Boron' minus 'Lawrencium' is equal to 'twin'.* So it would seem that Mi not only provided a word count process to connect Lawrencium and Mira but also provided the numbers of the two chemicals that produced Lawrencium.

I thus concluded that the connection between Lawrencium and Mira was established. Moreover I considered that we had found the focal point of the whole issue. On page 79 there is a diagram called the 'reaction chamber', which describes the Lawrencium and Mira Ceti connections.

However, this is not the end of the story and I revisit and revise this diagram later.

In an act of apparent selfishness (joke) the word count for Mi (or Dale) can also be derived from the sequential addition of 'Californium' and 'Boron is 17+5 = 22 = 'Dale' (or 'Mi).

I share my Christian name with my father, as does my own son, so there are three generations of Lawrence within my recent

Chapter 8 – What's in a name?

family. Now, I don't know how many Lawrence Dales there must be in England, quite a few, I suspect. Of course the field could be narrowed down a bit by finding those who have a father of the same name, and then again by finding those who have an existing son of the same name. I would think that this narrows the field down a lot, but I would imagine there are still quite a few. Would my mother's name be involved?

There is quite an involved complication here, and we need to explain this before continuing. It is important, because as mentioned earlier, we have to be as objective and truthful as we can, so it becomes necessary explore to these issues.

My mother and father were never actually married by ceremony. My mother had been married before, her married name then being Carr. Her original maiden surname was Knoweldon. It was apparently the choice of Mr. Carr to leave my mother for another woman and that he remarried and had another family. I understand my mother and father lived together for years before my birth, but Mr. Carr could not have remarried unless there had been an official divorce between him and my mother. Yet I could not find records of this (having checked some years back).

What complicated the issue further was that official people also used my mother's Maiden name. I was told by official sources that before my birth, 'some office' had deemed that Mr. Carr and my mother, having been separated for so long and each being with new partners, would be considered as divorced. After consultation with the War Office it was decided that my mother's surname would be Dale. It is also possible that Insurance issues were brought to bear on this. It is unlikely that today, such a thing would be permissible. Anyway, both commonly and officially my mother was known as Dale.

My mother's Christian name was Elizabeth. However I have also considered the value of previous surnames, just for completeness. I did not expect to find any connection but to my surprise three possible links were found.

Knoweldon = 113 and 41, Carr = 40 and 22. 41 and 22 occur in both Mira and Mi (or Dale), though we must admit these are by crossing the arithmetic and sequential procedures. Another point is that adding all sequential values for the three surnames equals the sequential figure for the last surname of Dale and creates another set of three*. This might suggest the name Dale is confirmed. Birth years also contain coincidences, but I consider these later.

The count for the acronym BUFORA is 63 and that of Thailand is 69. These remain important places of contact between Norman and me because we first met when I joined BUFORA and our relationship became more personal when Thailand became involved. The average of these two numbers is 66, Norman's term for the double pupils of the Mi image.

Looking at the revised 'reaction chamber' diagram we can see a central figure of 144 and by coincidence 'Norman' plus 'Thailand' equals 144. The country sequential counts, Thailand plus England is equal to BUFORA and Lawrencium plus Thailand plus Mira equals the count for 'Dale'. Crossing the addition systems once again, the sequential count for Lawrence William Dale added to the count for Mira, is equal to the count for Omicron Ceti.*

Adding Ceti in English to Thai Ceti equals the Atomic number for Lawrencium (103 in *any* language) because the word Ceti in Thai the same count for 'Twin' in English, 66. Since 103 can mean my name also, it seems that I am connected to Mira.

Adding the counts for Twin and Mira Ceti the result is the same as the 'glue' number of the 'reaction chamber' diagram, 144. Thailand and Norman being mentioned previously my conclusion then was that both were 'connected' and this latter sum seems to support that. Could the birthdates (see page 9) represent the count for Thailand using three times 23? Another strange coincidence occurs when adding together the sequential numbers of 'Norman', 'Thailand' and 'Cat', where the result is the count for Thailand. This would support the earlier inference.

Some other possibilities were found this way but have not been included because I am not convinced the procedure is valid. The above paragraphs show that such avenues were explored. However, most connections remain as already described. (You may have read that recent Crop Circles 'reply', where the product of the two prime numbers 73 and 23 was used in the original outgoing SETI signal. Not only is the sequential number for Mira represented in the primes, but the sequential value of the product also gives Mira's sequential value.)

Could it be possible that as I was living in Thailand when contact was made with Mi, that the Thai language might also be involved? I thought not, but then having had the thought, why not do some sums just for completeness? More coincidences were found and I had to revise the 'Reaction Chamber'.

Though both the English and Thai languages have an alphabet, they are quite different in structure. For example, the Thai language has more than one character for the sound 'T' and this goes for 'K', 'P' and other sounds. In addition to this, as well as the many given vowels there are also spoken but unwritten ones.

Though the Thai word for 'person' or 'you' is usually written in English as 'khun', this should more correctly be 'khon', as shown in dictionaries used by Thai colleges and schools. ('khun' is the polite address when *speaking* to another person.) This gives the addition of KH+O+N. In fact, written in Thai, the 'O' vowel does not appear so, written in English it would be 'khn'. It often happens with the vowel 'a' in the same way. I have used the **full** Thai alphabet; many dictionaries do not list the unwritten vowels. To my utter surprise, this first attempt resulted in a connection. Comparing the word count for Lawrencium in English and in Thai (taken from a Thai dictionary: 103 is constant in any language being the atomic number) and then adding the answer is the sum of the two alphabets, 85 + 26. Oh dear! Look what happens when we add it all together – 666!*

[Page 73† this is not true and corrected in another book]

*

Bottom of page 74; Thor + Odin = 103, Trio + Mira = 103 and Elizabeth Dale + Lawrencium, 43+13+47 = 103.

Page 75 2nd paragraph; Omicron Ceti = 87+37 = 124, page 75; 222-124 = 98, Boron connects to Mira 41 = 4 +1 = 5 and 23, 2+3 = 5. 'Californium' + 'Boron' - 'Lawrencium' = 'twin', 121+64-119 = 66. Bottom page 78; 111+230+103+222=666

(Continued on page 80)

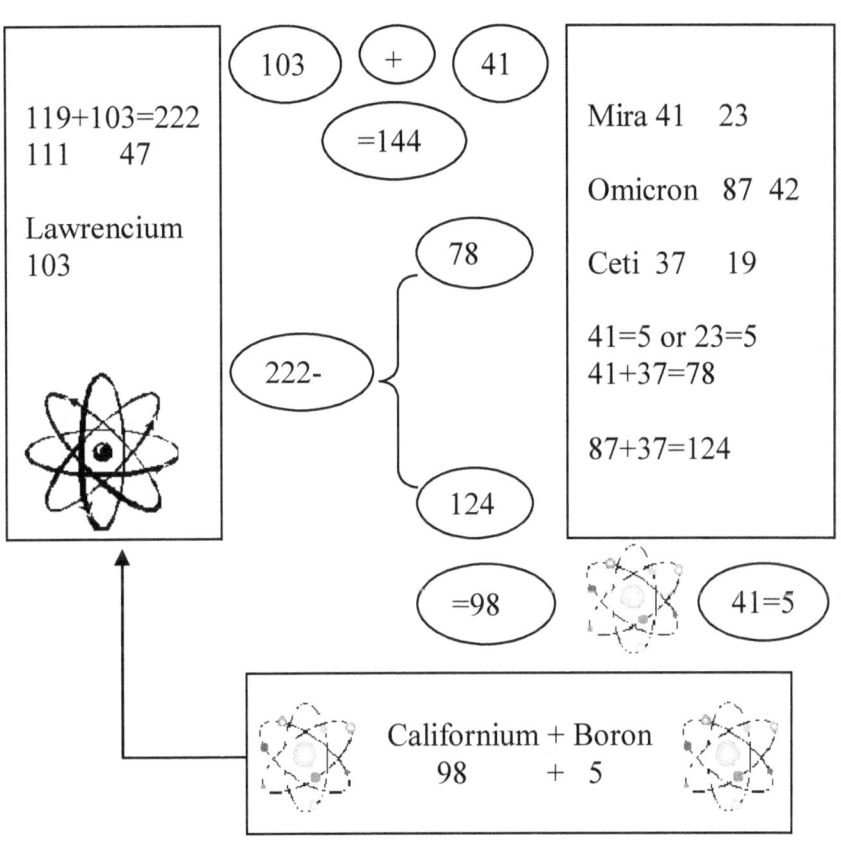

119+103=222
111   47

Lawrencium
103

103 + 41

=144

78

222-

124

Mira 41   23

Omicron 87 42

Ceti 37   19

41=5 or 23=5
41+37=78

87+37=124

=98   41=5

Californium + Boron
98   + 5

Chapter 8 – What's in a name?

Three sixes; could this mean 6 and 3 are interchangeable in some way? The answer is 'yes' and this suggests that there is a connection between the English and Thai counts with regard to Mira and Lawrencium or myself. However, because Norman and I are both Englishmen it is reasonable that we should find more connections using the English language.

On page 83 is the 'Reaction Chamber revisited' and this diagram shows the connection between Mira Ceti and Lawrencium in relation to both English and Thai languages.

So at this point, we have established connections between the words and names within the post experience analysis and we perhaps have gone as far as we can with this process. However, what we have failed to do is to find what we were aiming for at the beginning of this chapter – Mi's whereabouts. Admitted that we have the constellation Cetus and the star Mira, but Mira is not so far away that our present technology would not be able to detect something. I have concluded that both Lawrencium and Mira are fundamental to the issue, but, at present they give no information about Mi. Having derived numbers from names, what if we now reverse the procedure? This will be the subject of the next chapter.

A theory.

There appears to be one final coincidence to consider.

None of the names and words considered so far are of our own procuring, that is, Norman and I had no influence, even where our own names are concerned. From the experience we moved on to the star Mira Ceti due to the coincidences of the Latin word 'mira'. With other coincidences that were not originally linked to Mira Ceti, such as Lawrencium, we find a word count connection between them.

How could all these 'coincidences' happen with a specific experience involving just a minute part of the language? And how could it be that someone, or something, knew enough about these to stimulate their being found?

The only way that this could have happened is if the English language or perhaps certain parts of it were deliberately influenced by agencies other than those considered as being natural

Chapter 8 – What's in a name?

evolution. In addition, it would seem that it was not an arbitrary influence. It may be that at least parts of our language have been deliberately engineered, so that the construction of old words with new ones, or the construction of new words, would follow some pre-planned trend.

One may ask as to WHY other agencies would want to do this? What would they gain? One very good reason for doing this may be considered in the following example.

Supposing that we give another animal species with comprehension capabilities, such as apes for example, three basic figures to work with, say:

Now of these, combinations of the square and the triangle might be considered less advanced than combinations with the circle, because they have definite apexes, or angles that might bear some relationship. Tilting the triangle on its side to give one perpendicular side, opening the opposite angle, making the other two lines parallel to each other, then joining the gap with a fourth line, would reproduce the square. This process would have to be repeated many times to achieve the circle.

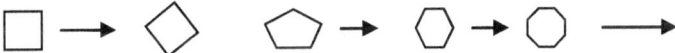

This would actually allow us to check the ape's progress. Another good example of this is the car. The original ones were like boxes on wheels, whereas many of the present day cars are aerodynamically designed. Tracking each shape can tell us what period a particular design belongs to and If our language was engineered in some way, it could have been for this very reason.

So it might be that Mi was aware of such influence but then again suppose Mi was NOT aware of this. *Was* Mi 'contacting me' simply an arbitrary choice? This, then, raises a very big question – where did all these connections come from? The answer may be

Chapter 8 – What's in a name?

that they came from an agency that even influenced Mi in making a choice, and that Mi was unaware of this.

Be that as it may, I think *we* must consider that Mi knew what the situation was and selected me for some particular reason. This being difficult enough as it is, for us to consider anything beyond Mi may be impossible.

In any research there is the hard work, often surprises and also humorous interventions. In 1991, I purchased a plaque with the history of the name Dale. During the time of flooding in Thailand many things were packed away and that was one of them, and after redecoration I left it packed away. With all this research I was doing I decided to find it. It seems that the first **recorded** 'Dale' was on the London 100 scrolls in the year 1273, and was one Ralph de la Dale, a native of Norfolk. Dale and 'de la' amount to the same, letter wise. In addition to that, the year 1273 when added sequentially gives 13, the sequential number of Dale. One wonders if there is a Lawrence Mi Dale tucked away in history somewhere. Just joking!

Stranger still is the coincidence that in one of my chemistry books, *Introduction to Physical Chemistry*, by G. I. Brown, S.I. Edition 1975, the number of the page that refers to the production of Lawrencium is page number 141, which matches Lawrencium, 119 added to Dale, 22. One just has to smile.

*

Top of page 76; 41+22+13 = 13.
Middle of page 77; ...revised 'reaction' chamber = 144. Norman and Thailand, 75 + 69 = 144. Country sequential counts Thailand + England 30 + 33 = 63, Lawrencium + Thailand + Mira 47+33+23=22. Crossing systems, Lawrence William Dale, 36+34+13 = 83, plus Mira, 41, equals 124.
Bottom page 78; English 119+103 = 222, Thai 230+103 = 333

Chapter 8 – What's in a name? 'reaction chamber' revisited

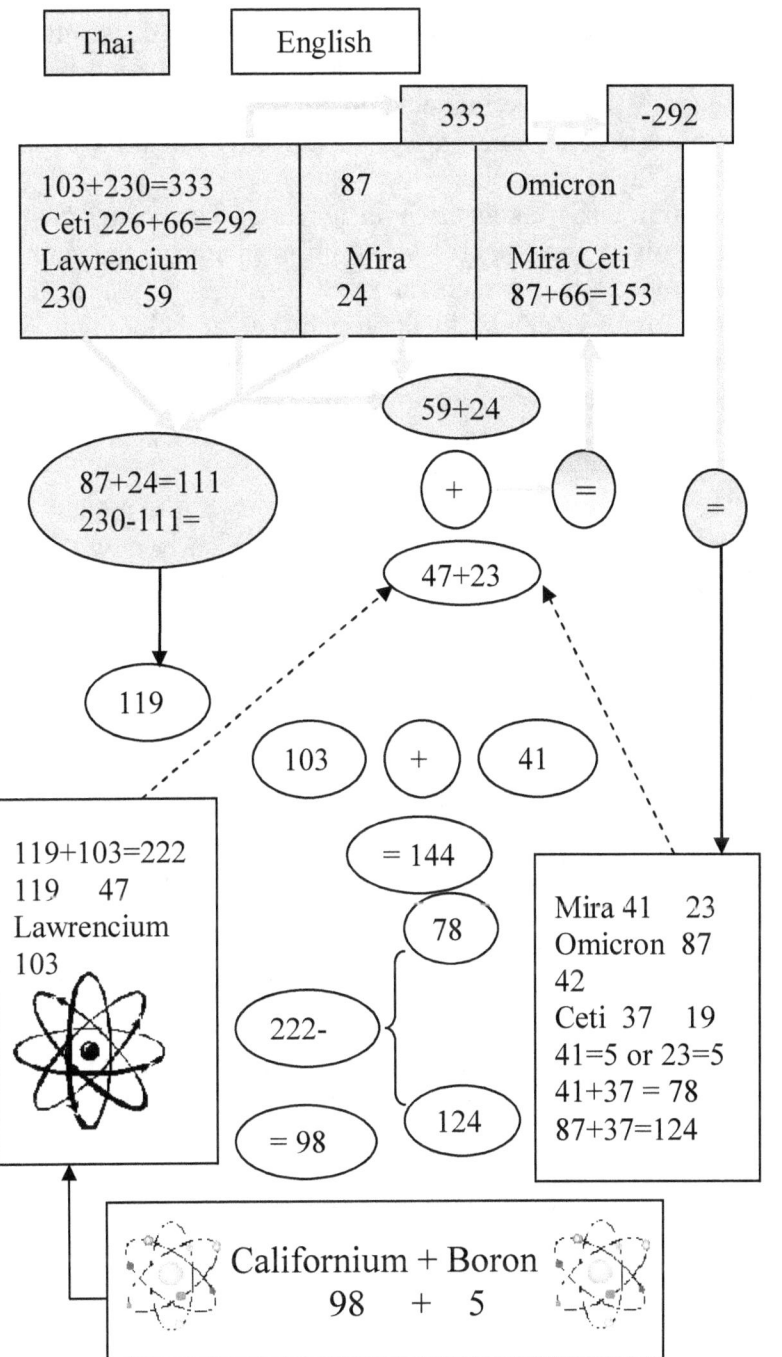

Thai

English

333

-292

103+230=333
Ceti 226+66=292
Lawrencium
230   59

87

Mira
24

Omicron

Mira Ceti
87+66=153

59+24

87+24=111
230-111=

+

=

=

47+23

119

103   +   41

119+103=222
119   47
Lawrencium
103

= 144

78

222-

= 98

124

Mira 41   23
Omicron 87
42
Ceti 37   19
41=5 or 23=5
41+37 = 78
87+37=124

Californium + Boron
98   +   5

Chapter 9 – All at sea with Enki

In the preceding chapters we have looked at all the 'coincidences' involved within the entirety of the experience itself and in the study that came immediately afterwards. However, what we might have here is similar to what a detective could have when investigating, say, a murder.

A murder has taken place in a house. The owner has an alibi at the given time; there was no forced entry; the murder weapon belongs to the owner. The dead person is known to have been in the employment of the house owner and Shouting was heard coming from the house prior to the estimated time of the murder. The house owner reported his car stolen a few hours before, and the car was seen outside the house at the time of the shouting.

The detective can arrest the house owner on suspicion, but in a court of law the detective knows that the suspect will walk free. Unless the detective can prove the alibi to be false, all he has is circumstantial evidence.

I had an experience where it seemed that no information was freely given and that in Norman's own words, nothing Earth shattering was obtained. I therefore remain the only person with the (and lack of) knowledge, that an event took place. Norman's own brief strange experience may be connected, but as Mi was not present we don't *actually* know if this is so. That Norman and I were connected both as friends and as in-laws (by marriage) is a strong coincidence but remains circumstantial.

The studies after the event again showed many connections, and I became convinced that they were 'leading' to some particular point, perhaps the meaning to it all. However, no such element became evident, and it was beginning to look as though that's how things would stay. There was no one thing that stood out by itself that could not be denied. It must be said that many of the points that linked together were more than just interesting to Norman and I – at times they were no less than fascinating. In the end, however, they all just seemed to confirm one another and not really lead *outside* of their own domain. Then, just by coincidence....

What I did was to take numbers derived from the names and performed mathematical procedures on them. Because of

84

Chapter 9 – All at sea with Enki

previous implications that the number 3 seemed important, I made the basic number equal to 3. With 'Lawrencium', for example, one procedure added 22 ('Mi' or 'Dale'?) to give a total of 141. In another example I multiplied each of the numbers from the counts of Lawrencium with the number counts from Mira, and the result is a number very close to the atomic number of Lawrencium (or Lawrence Dale), 103.14563.

A skeptic might argue that it is not a legitimate process to perform mathematics on names. Firstly I would point out that I have performed mathematics on the numbers, not the names. Secondly, why should any one object to this when companies and banks do this to our names every day? Lastly, I think the skeptic would be merely 'clutching at straws' because the answers speak for themselves.

However, what we have done here is to confirm what we had already suspected previously. Pleased as we are in finding that mathematics has confirmed our theory, we are still within the same domain. What we now need are answers that will extend outward and provide us with new knowledge.

It is true to say that for some reason I was more intrigued by the first result, the addition of 22. Perhaps because it could represent the word count for Dale or Mi, but having turned my mind to mathematics, 22 'rang a bell', so to speak

There were also a couple of other avenues to be explored, particularly the aim of the previous chapter. So, adding 24 (from Mi's '... to 24') to 119, 103, 41 and 37 we get 324. Not seeing anything direct in this number, I returned once more to the idea of 'a' through to 'x' and thinking of the 'reaction chamber' diagram, I looked for an obvious connection to the number 24. The most obvious one was 144, which I called the 'glue' number. This number had all the ingredients that the number 24 had plus one other. There are six 24s in 144.

I then numbered all the letters of the alphabet to the letter 'x', starting with $a = 6, b = 12, c = 18$ and so on until x = 144.*

Immediately one recognizes the numbers 78 and 66, though 103 or 119 are not represented – well, not immediately anyway. Not forgetting of course that $78 + 66 = 144$. Now, adding the two

Chapter 9 – All at sea with Enki

end numbers of the first row, 6+72 and then 12+66 and following this procedure we get 78 six times. Similarly for the second row the answer is 222 where by coincidence the sequential addition of 222 is 6. Just as a 'by the way' note here, the Binary code figure for 222 is 11011110, which contains six '1's, as does 119, 1110111. This seems to confirm that the counts for Mira Ceti and Lawrencium (plus Atomic number) are important.

We have just met the number 324, and using the 'a to x' group we can see that only *six* numbers here will divide exactly into 324, namely 6, 12, 18, 36, 54 and 108. Then there are *six* numbers in the sequence that have a sequential value of 6, namely 6, 24, 42, 60, 114, and 132. The 6<u>th</u> number here, 132, just happens to be equal to six time twenty two. The six numbers add up to 378, which when divided by 6 equals 63.

Now at this point we need to digress and regress a little because I had met this number 63 on two occasions before not as yet mentioned (remember that the count for 'BUFORA' is 63).

Adding Mira, 41 and Mi, 22, equals 63. Also I had added 24 to Ceti and Mira, which gave 61 and 65 respectively. Was there another word that I had not yet considered that would give yet another triad, 37, (?) and 41. I began looking for a word that would have a count of 39. One word I considered was 'mile'. Number-wise this fitted nicely as the following shows.

Mira 41, 23
Mile 39, 21
Ceti 37, 19

However nicely it fitted I really could not make sense out of the three words. So I e-mailed Norman and asked if he could find a word with a count of 39, though I did not tell him why I wanted it. After a day or two, Norman replied with Enki, which fitted just as 'mile' did, with counts of 39 and 21. However, what Norman had found meant much, much more than just the numbers. On the next page is an excerpt from a translation about Enki.

Chapter 9 – All at sea with Enki

'ENKI AND THE WORLD ORDER'
From *The Sumerians*, by Samuel Noah Kramer

"My father, the king of the universe, Brought me into existence in the universe. My ancestor, the king of all the lands, Gathered together all the me's, placed the me's in my hand.

I am the 'great storm' who goes forth out of the 'great below'. I am the lord of the Land. I am the GUGAL of the chieftains, I am the father of all the lands. I am the 'big brother' of the gods, I am he who brings full prosperity. I am the record keeper of heaven and earth. I am the ear and the mind (?) of all the lands. I am he who directs justice with the king An on An's dais. I am he who decrees the fates with Enlil in the 'mountain of wisdom'. He placed in my hand the decreeing of the fates of the 'place where the sun rises'. I am he to whom Nintu pays due homage. I am he who has been called a good name by Ninhursag. I am the leader of the Anunnaki. I am he who has been born as the first son of the holy An.

My magur-boat dispensing from sunrise to sunset the me's to (?) the people. Your me's are lofty me's, unreachable."

One can immediately notice in the second and third lines the term 'me's'. It turns out that the 'me' were something similar to the Ten Commandments of Christianity. Some sources put Enki as a sea God, and something like this is also implied above when speaking of " My magur-boat".

So Norman not only found a word that fitted in with the numbers, but the implications about the sea fitted in with the constellation Cetus. Not only that, what amounts to an astonishing coincidence is the term 'me' (but see the *Epilogue* concerning a mistake here) connected to Enki, and that this book is about the Mi experience. Enki had another name and it was Ea, again was associated with water and the word counts for Ea, 6 and sequential count of 6 (exactly the same as 'cat').

So I had another name to consider, indeed I would be foolish not to, given the above implications. With the number '6'

Chapter 9 – All at sea with Enki

occurring so much it was hard to ignore, and, once again, it rang a bell. Incidentally, when adding 6 to the count of 'Norman' we get 81, which is the same as the count for 'Oliver' or 'Lawrence'

I had claimed previously that Lawrencium and Mira Ceti were central to the issue and looking at some counts for Mira Ceti the number six turns up again, twice.* In addition to this as was shown in the 'reaction chamber' diagram, Californium 98 and Boron 5 were the two elements that produced Lawrencium and the result is twenty two.* The numbers 22 and 6 seemed to have a meaning.

One of the most useful 'constants' in mathematics is π, Pi, and every school student knows this is 22÷7 or 3.143. Actually, the value of π is closer to 22÷7.0028, and in fact my computer gives the value of

3.1415926535897932384626433832795

(I personally use a value of 3.14159265. Computation of decimal places usually stops when sets of numbers reoccur, but in the case of π no one has yet to be found it.)

So this was the reason why the continuous thoughts of 22 seemed familiar.

It would seem that we arrive at a new Factor (22÷6) = 3.666666667 to nine decimal places. One can see that the original thought that the number 3 was important is also contained here as eleven thirds, (11÷3)

The constant π is well established in circular or periodic calculations and is not likely to be replaced by some other number, certainly not 3.666666667. However, **if** Mi intended for me to deduce 3.666666667, what possible use could it have? Even more mysterious is that Mi claimed that Mi life did not use numbers. Why then deduce a number? I suppose the only answer can be that I would have not understood anything else.

Using this new number on some of the previous work involving 'Mira', we get an answer of 81, which as I have just mentioned above, just happens to be the word count for Lawrence and Oliver. Even more surprising is the addition of 1273 and 99 (Ralph de la Dale from page 82) divided by the new number gives 374.1818..., very close to Norman's full name count.

Chapter 9 – All at sea with Enki

Having introduced Enki and the new factor, this is perhaps the most convenient place to consider some family details. In considering both Norman's and my parents' names we notice that between the six people, the surnames combine and gives a result which could be interpreted as three times the Atomic number for Lawrencium (103).

Next, notice that when the year of birth for Norman and me is added the answer is 68 which is the name count for Cetus. Even if we go about it in a completely different way, we end up with the same figure. Or to put it another way, in 1968 Norman was 42 years old and I was 26.

What we really need to find is a family 'coincidental connection', since this would establish some kind of 'root'. We do not have to look far.

Obviously, with my family the coincidence is to 'Mi', the surname 'Dale' has the same word count. In this way one might say that it was pre-ordained that I would be a candidate for contact with the entity Mi.

The (married) name count of Norman's mother is exactly six times that of 'Enki', and his father's word count is four times 'Enki' plus one divided by 'Enki'. Once again it seems to have been 'pre-ordained' that Norman should be involved with the number 39. Where is that all-important bridge?

Norman's name count divided by Enki (39) does not give a familiar figure, but when divided by 22 (Mi) it equals 17. 17 is my father's birthday and the difference in years of both our fathers birth years, 1884 and 1867. However, Norman's name count *is* nine times 'Enki' plus 39 divided by 23 and 23 you will remember is the number involved with the birthdates of my mother and my wife (see page 9).

Considering the difference of our two mothers' birth years, 1887 and 1902, 15 years, just happens to be the mirror image of the above addition of the three 17s, 51. Adding the mirror image numbers together equals sixty six, which just happens to be the word count for 'twin' which Norman also introduced into this analysis. However the plot thickens so to speak because 1887 is equal to forty eight times 'Enki' plus **15** divided by 'Enki' and

Chapter 9 – All at sea with Enki

1902 is equal to forty eight times 'Enki' plus two times 15 (that is 30) divided by 'Enki'. These findings along with 309 mentioned previously, I conclude that the 'coincidental bridge' has been exposed.

Now it becomes possible to use another figure I had computed, but without any usefulness. In terms of millennia I had previously calculated that 1.914854216 millennia squared equals the factor (22÷6). Since both Norman's and my year produce results way outside of the factor, some kind of 'buffer' would seem to be required. Using my mother's year with Norman's and Norman's mother's year with mine, achieves results of 99.91% and 99.94% of (22÷6) respectively. With the inclusion of our fathers' years the average of the 'crossing over of parents' results is 99.4% of (22÷6), and for the direct family results is 99.43% of (22÷6).

With these figures, and those mentioned earlier for Enki and the factor, I am now convinced of our connection to Mi and Enki. However, there is one qualifying note here. I do not conclude that this is unique. What I conclude is that OUR generation is connected to (22÷6). What may be possible is that, along with certain other considerations, our figures may have come closer to (22÷6) for the needs of Mi in making a choice.

When looking at our parents' name counts and crossing the implied connection to Mi and Enki the new factor can be derived. Using my mother's name with the factor, the number 24 can be derived. A second factor has also been derived from the first.

What about Mira Ceti and Lawrencium? 'Mira Ceti' plus 'Lawrencium (plus 103)' times 'Mi' = 6600, which is reminiscent of Norman's 'twin',66. Divide 6600 by the new factor and the answer is 1800, exactly the figure obtained by adding together the six 78's and six 222's from page 86.

The numbers and the computations cannot be disputed. The factors, which I have named 'Tridel 1' and 'Tridel 2', have highlighted a large number of numerical coincidences, as well as coincidences in Chemistry and Physics. My interpretation is that with we have come full circle and back to where it all began. It is for you, the reader, to decide upon your own interpretation. (My

Chapter 9 – All at sea with Enki

mathematical symbols for Tridel 1 and Tridel 2 are $^{\equiv}\partial$ and $_2^{\equiv}\partial$ respectively. In Part 3 where I have used just the word 'Tridel', this refers to Tridel 1.)

We can look at this in the perspective of the Martial Arts. Many believe that when a student has obtained a Black Belt, that is the end of the Road. It isn't. Actually, a new learning process begins which takes the student much further. Similarly, with my continued study of the experience, I believe that I have learnt much more.

*

> Bottom of page 85
> a to x
> 6 12 18 24 30 36 42 48 54 60 66 72
> 78 84 90 96 102 108 114 120 126 132 138 144
>
> Top of page 88
> Mira Ceti, 41+23+37+19 = 5+5+10+10 =
> 5+5+1+1,
> Born & Californium 98+5 = 17+5 = 22.
>
> Page 89-90
> Family surnames, (22+81)×3 = 309
> Birth years 19261942=34,
> (1926+1942)÷2 = 1934, 1934+34 = 1968.
> Norman's father 157= 39×4+(1÷39),
> Norman's mother, 234 = 39×6,
> Norman's name = 374 =9×39+(39÷23)

Part 3 – Chapter 10 – Learning our ABCs'

In this chapter I will examine Mi's answers to my two equations and try to give a representation and explanation of Mi's other ideas. These representations must be viewed as approximate since I was unable to fully understand all of the content Mi gave me.

Also in this section I will further analyze the information as an attempt to reveal Mi's meaning of up to 24, etc. This has involved some mathematical work, but these details will not be given in this volume.

However, I have assumed in so doing, that in some way, Mi imparted to me all the necessary information to achieve these ends. I have also assumed that Mi must have known how Norman and I would think, and therefore knew the routes we would take during our efforts. As you read on, it would seem that Mi went further than this, and provided us with more than one route to achieve certain results. Thus, the 'explorations' in this section are an attempt to make some discoveries, and to some degree this has been achieved.

On page 94 is a representation of Mi's answer to my first equation set question. My own mathematical solutions will be presented in Volume 2.

It is interesting to note that Mi only gives the answer for one variable, y, whereas in our system both answers, $x = 2$, $y = 1$ would be required.

The number of 'cubes' in the diagram indicates the corresponding absolute number in the equation, i.e. 3 and 1. Three 'cubes' are on one side while a lone 'cube' is on the opposite side. The vertical parallelogram represents the 'Y' axis while the horizontal one is the 'X' axis. As I understood it the vertical became horizontal when two 'cubes' were deleted leaving two horizontals and two 'cubes'. This resulted in one horizontal being related to one 'cube'.

As I mentioned previously, this was quite simple and so I made the second question a little more complicated. On the next page I repeat the formulae given to Mi.

Chapter 10 – Learning our ABCs'

$$3a + 4b - 2c = 4$$
$$5a + 2b + 3c = 10$$
$$4a - 3b + 4c = 15$$

In the pages after those of equation set 1, there are the three sets of Mi's representations for the answer of the second equation set.

The difference in the two questions was that the first equation set gave results in whole numbers while the second set gave results with fractional parts, as well as being slightly more complex. Diagrams show Mi's representation, where the equation inserts illustrate what each part represents in our terminology. Once again, the objects shown are not accurately drawn, and there were colors also present in the originals. The area of the ellipses represents the right hand side of the equations. The arrows represent the three different coefficients of 'a', 'b' and 'c', while the black arrows represent the negative sign. The position of the arrows, as far as I am aware, is not significant. It must be remembered that these diagrams are over simplifications, as I was unable to convey the other properties that seemed to be present. There seemed to be some continuous type of movement that I was unable to control, although it may be possible that this feature was a characteristic of my own mind. The vertices that are shown are by no means accurate, but it is the only representation that comes close.

A representation of Mi's answer to my first equation set.

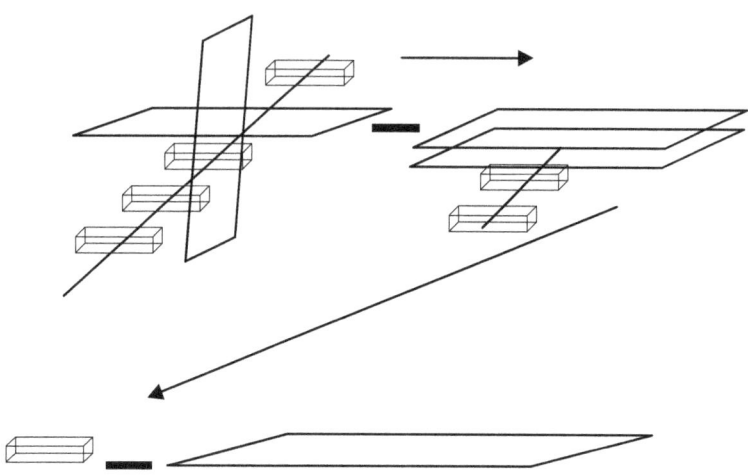

In the originals different colours were also given. The 3-D cubes were all of the same colour, The horizontal parallelograms were another colour and the other lines were also a different colour. The vertical parallelogram was the darkest colour [the arrows are mine].

Chapter 10 – Learning our ABCs'

Mi's answer to my second equation set, section 1.

The diagrams may require a little effort to understand but I ask that the general reader bear with me, not so much with my equations but the explanations of Mi's representations. One must also consider the possibility that the reader may 'see' something in the diagrams that I have missed or perhaps seen something similar somewhere.

Below is a representation from Mi, but I was unable to draw it to scale. The area of the ellipsoids represents the answer to each of my expressions, which I have inserted alongside Mi's representation.

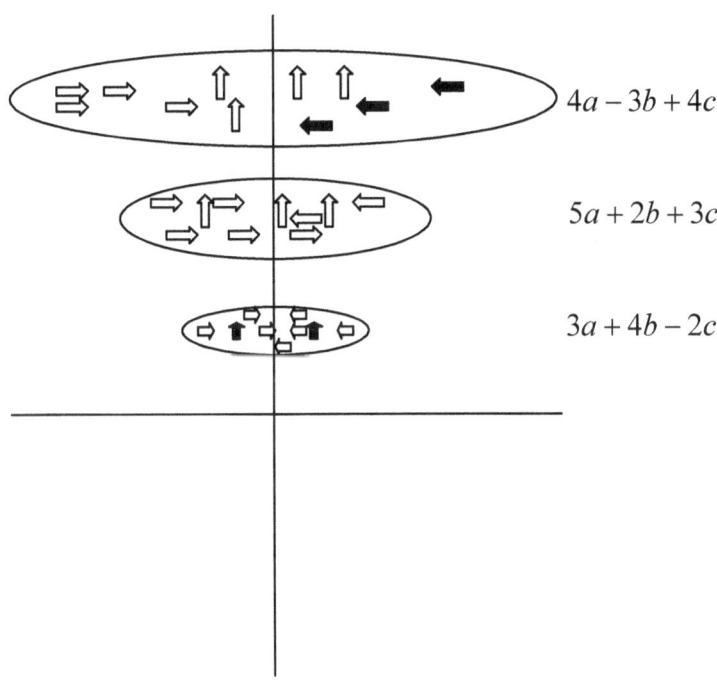

$$4a - 3b + 4c$$

$$5a + 2b + 3c$$

$$3a + 4b - 2c$$

Mi's answer to my second equation set, section 2.
Mi's next step was to insert additional ellipsoids and other shapes.

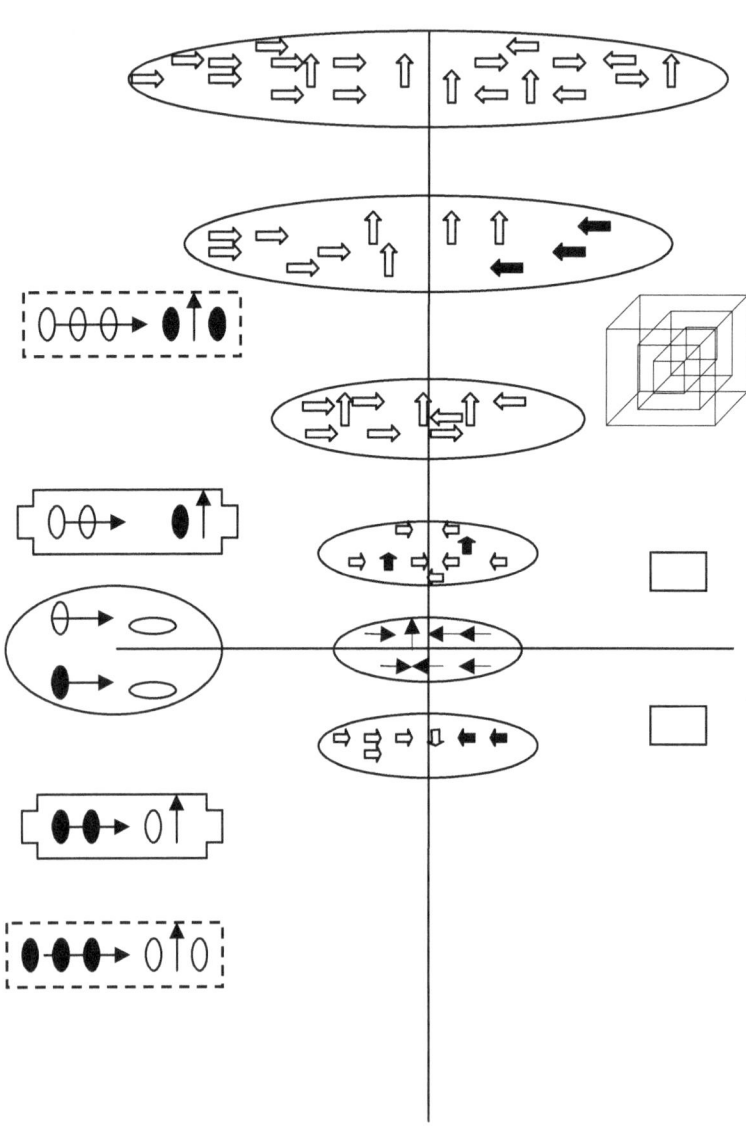

Chapter 10 – Learning our ABCs'

Mi's answer to my second equation set, section 3.
However, Mi's intermediate and final steps were anything but easy to work out, and I had to 'revisit the scene' as much as was permitted, as well as spending hours of using pencil and paper. The reason was that Mi inserted more shapes into the diagram above, below and to the sides of the 'vertices'. The arrangement of cubes on the right hand side of the top, largest ellipse represents all the three lines of equation 2 while the ellipse itself represents the combination of the three equation lines, i.e.

$$3a + 4b - 2c + 5a + 2b + 3c + 4a - 3b + 4c = 12a + 3b + 5c = 29$$

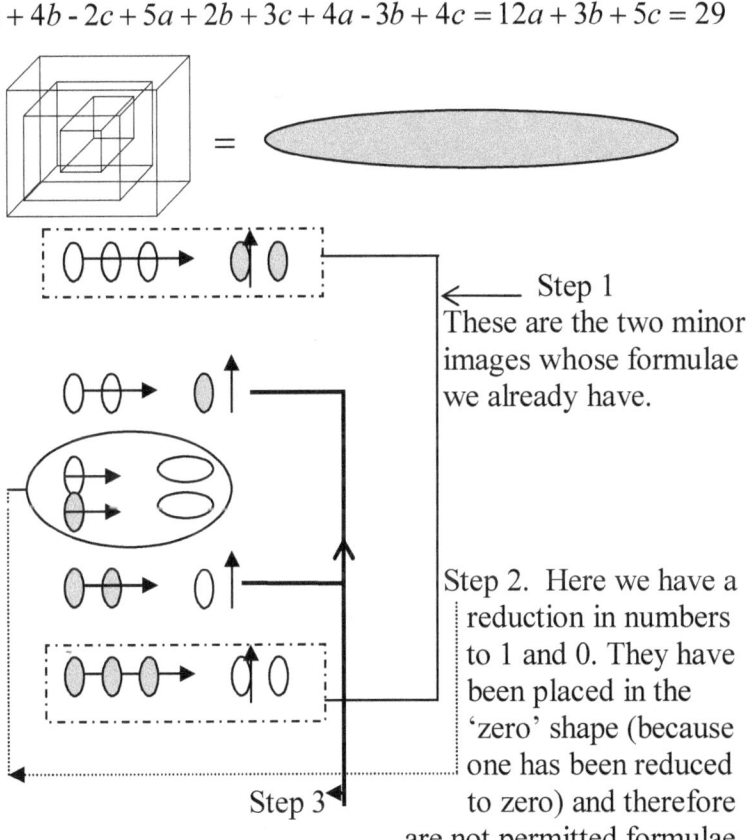

Step 1
These are the two minor images whose formulae we already have.

Step 2. Here we have a reduction in numbers to 1 and 0. They have been placed in the 'zero' shape (because one has been reduced to zero) and therefore are not permitted formulae.

Step 3.

Step 3. Here is a reduction of 1 in the numbers and the majority positive one is chosen. Algebraically-

Chapter 10 – Learning our ABCs'

$$-3a - 4b + 2c = -4$$
$$2a + 4b - c = 0$$
$$3a + 4b - 2c = 4$$
$$5a + 2b + 3c = 10$$
$$4a - 3b + 4c = 15$$
$$12a + 3b + 5c = 29$$

Just to make it as clear as I can I'll try to explain what 'Mi' is considering here. Along with the diagram below, on the following page is Mi's explanation of the 'steps' on the previous page.

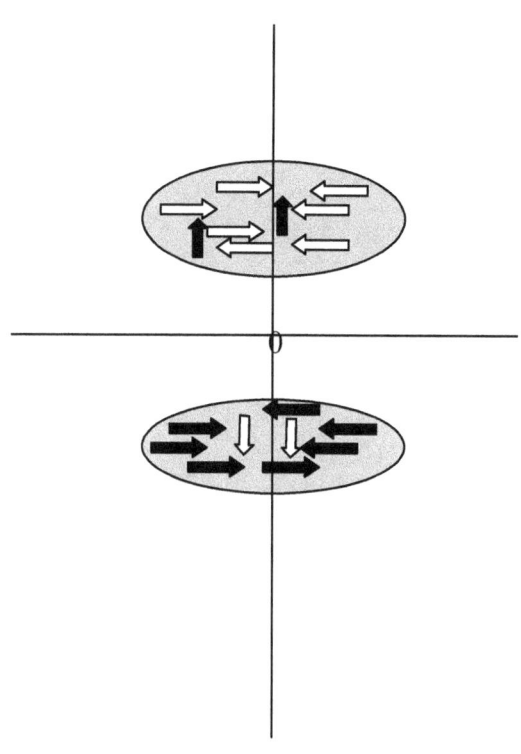

Chapter 10 – Learning our ABCs'

Mi wants get to get values on both sides of the zero point, keeping one term constant. It needs one term constant for a later procedure. Mi needs:

Something times (a) plus 4b plus something times (c) = 0

From the foregoing diagrams and equation list, zero is somewhere between the values $-3a$, $3a$, and $2c$, $-2c$. So decreasing the values by one progressively Mi obtains the values $-2a$, $2a$ and b, $-b$ and then $-a$, a, but b has now vanished. The values $1a$, $-a$, and $0b$, $-0b$ have no significance in this particular setting so Mi calls them 'no value consideration', which I have translated to '.....not permitted.....' on the previous page. Mi likes positive values so it chooses the formulae with the most positive items, hence the second equation on the previous page $2a + 4b - c = 0$.

The two rectangles on either side of the horizontal line are mirror images, and so the first line of the equation becomes $3a - 4b + 2c = -4$. This is not too hard to see, and seems to move along logically, but working it out took considerable time because of trying to find the meaning of the shapes on the left hand side of the diagram, containing the '0's' and 'arrows'.

These are Mi's 'explanation' shapes. The two outermost rectangles contain the mirror image mentioned before, and this is step 1. The next two inner shapes are actually step 3, where there is a reduction of 1 from the mirror images but the side with a positive majority is used. Those directly on the horizontal line represent what might be termed original total reductions and lie on the equivalent of a 'zero' point and therefore do not contain permitted [by Mi] formulae. The enclosing ellipse here represents a 'zero' entity. The '$+4b$' remains untouched. This is the second equation on the previous page $2a + 4b - c = 0$. The remaining explanations you will have already read with the diagrams.

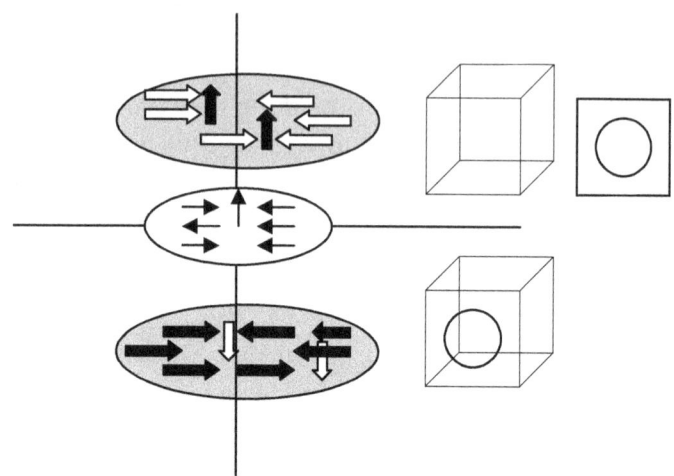

What Mi does next is to take away the '…= 0' line from the image and add the '…… = 0' line to the mirror image.

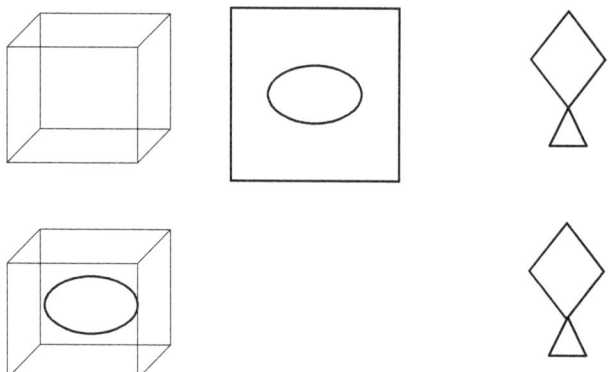

Chapter 10 – Learning our ABCs'

In our terms, algebraically (P1):

$$(3a + 4b - 2c) - (2a + 4b - c) = 4 - 0$$
$$(-3a - 4b + 2c) + (2a + 4b - c) = -4 + 0$$
$$(a - c = 4) \text{ and } (-a + c) = -4$$

Now at the top of page 97 I gave the representation of the addition of all three formulae lines of equation 2 giving the new line represented by the grey ellipse. Mi now adds this new line to the third (or bottom) line of the equation and gets a result involving the same two coefficients as in (P1) above.

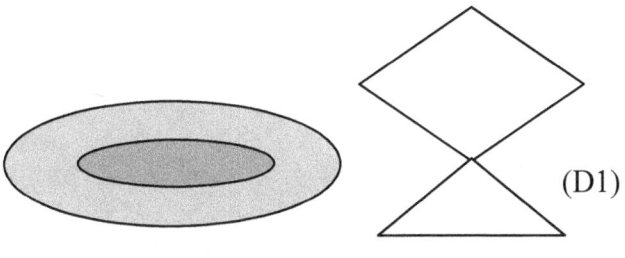

(D1)

$$(12a + 3b + 5c) + (4a - 3b + 4c) = 16a + 9c = 44 \ldots\ldots\ldots D1$$

Now Mi expands the positive result of (P1) to get (D2) until when added together the lower (orange actually) triangle exactly fits the lower (blue actually) triangle of (D1) and they cancel each other out in (D3). Since it is an addition the top shape is increased. This then represents in our terms, some number times 'a'= another number:

Chapter 10 – Learning our ABCs'

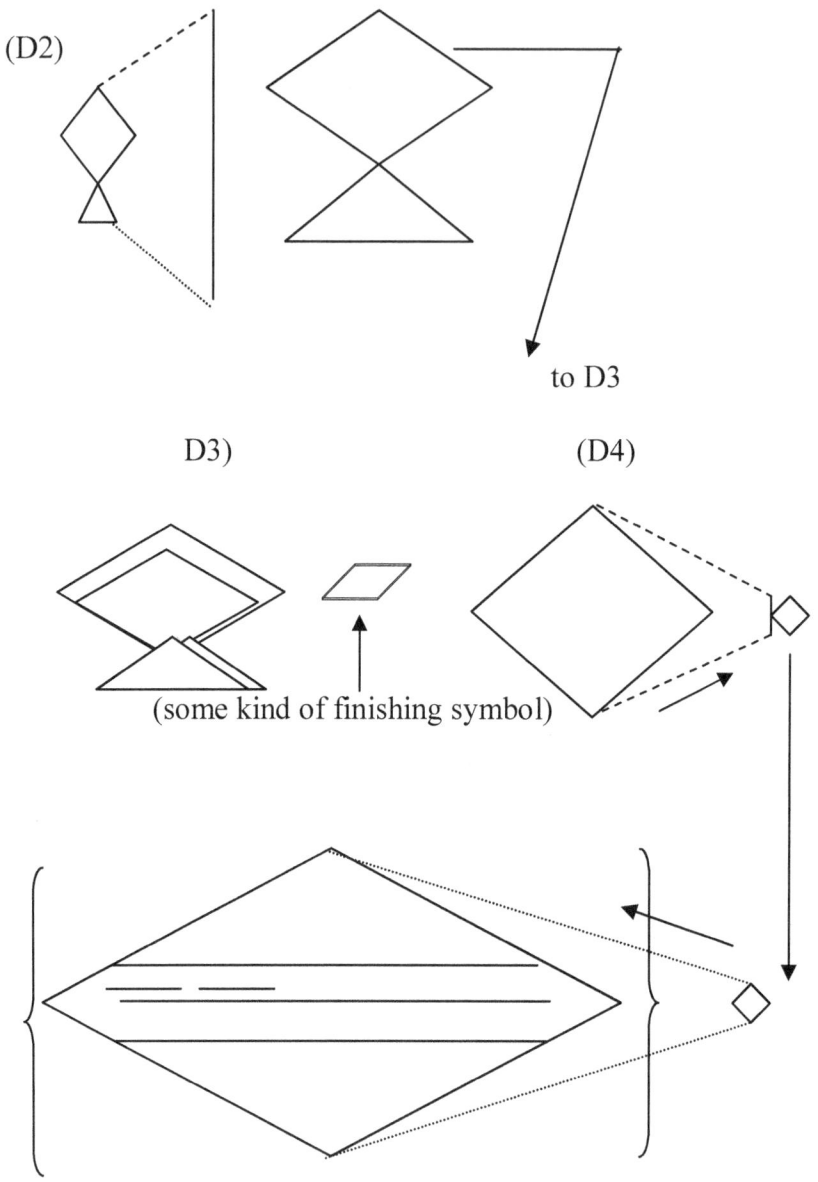

(D2)

to D3

D3)   (D4)

(some kind of finishing symbol)

So Mi has to decrease the size until it reaches unity. Actually, where I have used size Mi did not but was using some property. What about the last bit? Well I didn't understand what the final 'unity' was. So I asked for it to be given to me. In (D5) I considered it more than just a coincidence that the other 'shapes' inside the final shape resembled the final answer for 'a' in my computations as 3.2. Showing it algebraically and adding this to the result from page 101:

$$\left(\left(a-c\right)=4\right)\times 9 = 9a - 9c = 36, \left(16a + 9c = 44\right) + \left(9a - 9c = 36\right)$$
$$25a = 80 \therefore a = 80 \div 25 = 3.2$$

I must add that the above algebraic method of mine was criticized by Mi because Mi stated that my algebraic forms involved Negative Numbers and these don't exist. I think our Bank Managers might have something to say about that!

Further questions were related to other ideas, for example, that of Time. I will now look at some of Mi's ideas about Time, though later I will consider some further implications and analysis. For convenience I repeat some earlier comments.

As far as I was able to understand, Mi's idea of Time is very different from our own. In terminology that may not be completely accurate, Mi communicated ideas of 'Active' and 'Passive' Time. According to Mi, Now and the Past belong to Active Time while the Future is Passive Time. This might mean that in some way the areas of Now and the Past have become 'activated' while the Future remains 'Unactivated'. In addition to these three, Mi communicated the idea of a fourth Time area which also belonged to Passive Time. I can only loosely identify this as 'Unused' Time. This non-active Time can permeate the other three mentioned and also be external to them. Each of the four has different 'signatures', though this is capable of change and indeed does change, and it is this signature that is the 'Flowing' element of (Mi)Time. As one might expect, these ideas were not immediately acknowledged or understood by me.

Perhaps the idea of Now and the Past being 'activated' is not too difficult to accept, though one might not expect the Future to be inactive, for if it is inactive because it has not been used, why is it not the same as the Unused Time? Mi clearly defined them as

Chapter 10 – Learning our ABCs'

being different, hence my use of the term Passive to distinguish it from Unused. Is activated Time accessible? This is a question that we will discuss later.

I give here some analogies that might help in understanding the above concepts.

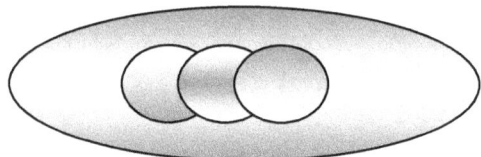

In the above diagram the 'Unused' Time is the larger ellipse while, from left to right are, Past, Now and Future Time. One should not view these in the same way that one might imagine the usual representation of the visible 'universe' as this would be misleading. While Stars, Galaxies etc. are dependent upon the space that they occupy, that is, they obey the laws within that space, the Time elements are not dependent on that space, nor are they dependent upon any other 'space'. Mi suggests that they are not confined within a 'space' and that they are co-ordinate free.

Our view of Time, Mi suggests, is not coordinate free inasmuch as we have labeled events in accordance with some periodic motion. For example, one revolution of the Earth about the Sun we define as one year, and we extend this to other events. Many of us tend to view clocks and other devices as giving us essential information about Time. Even in books about Time one reads these devices *measure* Time. In books on Mathematics one will read that Time is regarded as a *scalar* quantity, that is, possesses some magnitude but no unique direction. [Temperature is another scalar quantity. Some Force, on the other hand, is regarded as a vector quantity, because it not only possesses a unique magnitude, but also a definable direction.] Mi states that if *we* want to go back to some particular point, using *our definition* of time, we would need to literally move everything backwards.

Chapter 10 – Learning our ABCs'

Mi suggests that there is no 3-D Law that would permit us to move everything backwards. However, I must admit that there are some authors who **do** consider Time as being coordinate free. For example, performing an experiment today and obtaining a certain result, one would expect that in performing the same experiment tomorrow with identical materials, the result should be the same. In other words Time has not interfered with the outcomes. On the other hand, changing the order in which the items are used may well affect the outcome, so in this, the order is coordinate dependent.

This confirms what was said previously. Viewing Time as we do in everyday life we would need to move the coordinates backward to view some past event and that would mean affecting a major part of the universe and not just the coordinates we were interested in. In addition it would mean taking everyone else along too. This is obviously not what we want to do.

However, Mi does insist that everything produces its own record, but not in a coordinate dependent way. In other words, if one wants to view what one did yesterday, it is not necessary to consider the whereabouts of where one was.

This becomes confusing because how does one choose a particular period to view? Surely if one wants to view 10 a.m. yesterday morning the 24 hour coordinate frame would have to be used. Well, not so. If we lived on one of the other planets we would not be using a 24-hour frame. O.K. then, we can just use minutes, or seconds or some other form of measure to calculate back to the point we are interested in. Mi's point is that Active Time configures itself so that it forms an image of what has happened. Reconfiguration is possible, and apparently dangerous.

Mi states that while Mi has no real objection to the way we define our history, the objection is that we give (our version of) Time, properties, which by our own definition, it can't have. If we consider Time as a progressive movement from one state of affairs to another state, this definition rather lacks the salient point as to what happened to the previous condition, other than that it has changed. This definition says nothing about the property of Time being regressive, which would be essential for Time Travel.

Chapter 10 – Learning our ABCs'

Mi suggests that we are so entrenched in our 'historical' view of Time that we view these records as tangible evidence that our definition is correct. Mi says that there are other properties we need to consider to define otherwise.

With scientists presently working from Quarks to Massive Black Holes, it seemed to me that if there were an alternative definition or other properties, someone would have found it by now.

Diagram T1, I considered not quite accurate enough for the above definition from Mi so we need to look at more specific diagrams. These are Diagrams 5a & 5b.

Diagram 5a

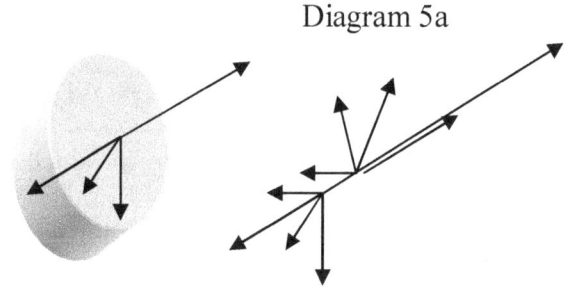

Diagram 5b

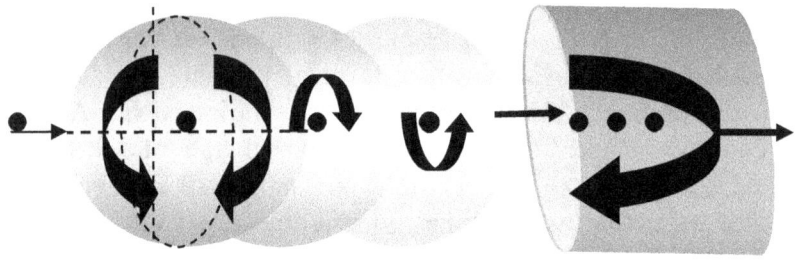

Diagram 5a is a reconstruction of Diagram 1 and there are extra 'arrows' added on the 'passage of time' arrow. These are what Mi calls 'collected time components'; Diagram 5b should be considered a more accurate description. The Electron, the black dot

Chapter 10 – Learning our ABCs'

is in its normal state within some system. When 'charged' it moves through that system, depicted here with spheres and a cylinder, and as it does so it also generates a magnetic field. For the present we will ignore this magnetic field. The electron also 'collects time components', the curved arrows, but because the electron does not 'use' these it leaves them 'behind'. A rough analogy might be to roll a metal ball bearing along the floor under a piece of cloth. As the bearing moves it hits and pushes the cloth out of the way. Hitting the cloth would be 'collecting' while pushing the cloth away would be leaving 'behind'. There may be a closer analogy but we will not include it here. Mi says that the electron has an Active C.T. system.

One wonders about the electron itself. Does the electron actually combine with, or is it permeated by the C.T.?

The electron mentioned above will have it's own C.T. signature. The atom in which the electron is a part will also have it's own signature. What is not clear however, is this; does every electron in every atom have a different C.T. signature, and does every atom of the same species, Oxygen say, have a different C.T. signature? Today, scientists have found no evidence at all to support this view, in fact quite the opposite. Indeed, electrons appear so identical that there is a theory suggesting the existence of only one electron. (If there was only one electron then this could have it's own signature. I am not suggesting I subscribe to this view, but just noting it.)

Electrons behave with a dual 'personality'. They behave in a particle manner and with wave properties. It seems here that the wave property is more in line with the C.T. signature.

Now, atoms combine with each other to eventually become, say, some cell in our body, which will have a C.T. signature. The position that the cell finds itself, say some organ, will have a C.T. signature. The situation in which that organ resides also has a C.T. signature. Thus by the time we end up with a human being we have a complex series of C.T. signatures, all different, yet with the whole having it's own C.T. signature.

Maybe this is not as crazy as it seems. Think of a situation between two people where they seem to 'click' with each other,

Chapter 10 – Learning our ABCs'

even at some distance apart. It is love at first sight. Why does this happen? Some scientist or biologist may say it is because of our Pheromones, chemicals that act at a distance. While this might be so in some cases I can think of several others where Pheromones would have extreme difficulty in getting through. Some believe it is Brain Wave patterns that are responsible, and yet others that suggest that it's simply 'survival of the species' at work; some might say it is a mixture of all of these. However, Love still remains to be defined satisfactorily in a real physical sense but could it be our 'signature' of Magneto-Time that is responsible? When it is compatible with someone else's 'signature' they interlock, when they actually repel, perhaps this is Hate. Is it also possible that we can change our 'signature'? Not everybody experiences a '…at first sight' relationship.

No, this is not going to turn into a 'counseling session'. The point I am trying to make is that of our feelings in general. Though there is no intention to debate this, how many of us have felt at some time or another that our feelings and conscience exist on another 'plane'.

I have drifted away from the idea of Time a little, so that I can now discuss something about Mi's ideas concerning perception processes.

This brings us to Mi's description of some of the processes involved in determining the position of an object. Once again, I am sure there are some inaccuracies in my attempt to explain this, but the general idea is basically demonstrated. In the following pages I offer more diagrams with an effort to retaining a three dimensional point of view.

On the next page, diagram 6 shows the usual way for us to give the position of a point, ●, in a local space. We use the Rectangular Coordinates 'x', 'y' and 'z'. This is just about as simple as one can get. It is clear and unambiguous and I doubt whether there is anyone who could not understand this.

Chapter 10 – Learning our ABCs'

Diagram 6

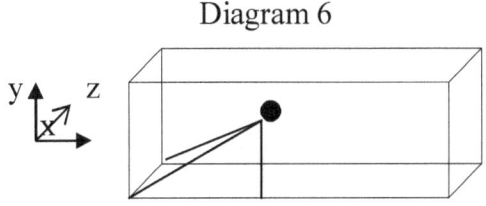

Diagram 7

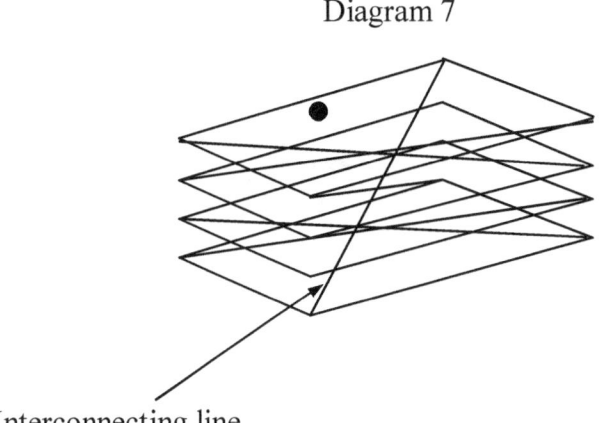

Interconnecting line

Diagram 8   Diagram 9   Diagram 10

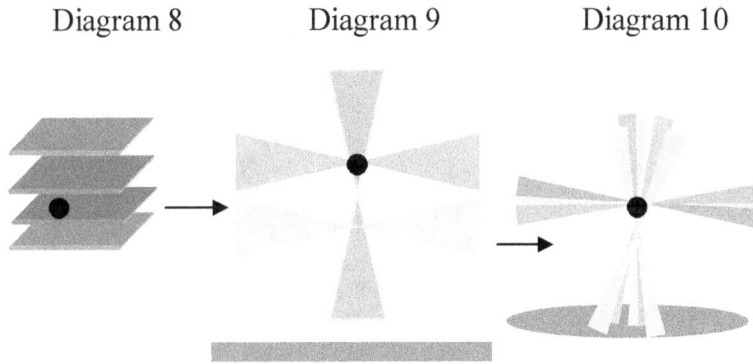

Chapter 10 – Learning our ABCs'

Diagram 11

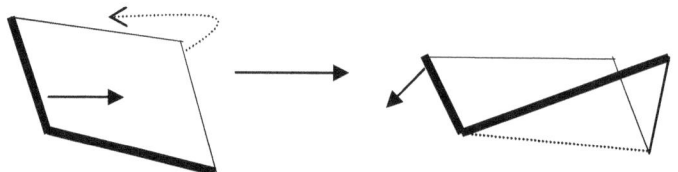

Diagram 12a

Diagram 12b

Chapter 10 – Learning our ABCs'

Take your memory back to the time when England changed its system to fit other international systems using the decimal scale where Twenty Shillings, £1, became 100 Pence. Road signs were supposed to have change to Kilometers, though even today Miles are still in use. Scientists have long used the decimal system and so there was no need to change here. One mile is approximately 1.6 kilometers, and is a relatively easy number to use for conversion. However, when we start considering Feet and Inches things become a little less certain. One Inch equals 2.54 Centimeters and One Meter equals 39.37...inches. Not to forgetting weight, One Pound equals 0.4537...Kilograms.

The point here is, if we convert from one system to another we must ensure that we understand the transformation equation that explains how to change from one system to another. For example, the transformation equation for changing Old pence into the Decimal pence of £1 is $2.4 \times 1^{Op} = 1^{Np}$. In this example £1 describes the position of the basic unit, just like the point in diagram 6. We could use any other system to define £1, but the position '£1' is not going to change.

In diagram 6, the situation is similar. We could change to *Polar* coordinates to describe the position of the point, using the angles and degrees, instead of distances from an origin. Indeed, when looking at a World map which uses Longitude and Latitude, we go a stage further and we are now into *Curvilinear* coordinates to describe curved space.

Now, none of this conflicts with our senses. We cannot take a straight ruler and measure the distance between, say, London and Edinburgh, because the surface of the Earth is curved. Of course a curved line from A to B is longer than a straight line from A to B. This is why map designers put the differences at the beginning – 1 inch = 1.2 miles, or whatever conversion they have used.

So with regard to diagram 6, if we use a curved system to identify the position of the point, the distances will be different while the position of the point itself is unchanged. As long as we stay in the safe local area there is no problem but once we move out of the local area and start considering other factors to which the point might also be related, things are not so simple.

Chapter 10 – Learning our ABCs'

Going back to the £1, as long as we stay with British currency, all is well. However, if we start to consider the position of the £ with regard to the $ one finds that what may be the £ of today is indeed not in the same position as it was yesterday, yet no one in Britain would have actually moved the position of the £. The £ is unchanged with regard to Britain, but has changed *relative to* the $.

So the essential term here is '*relative to*'. In diagram 6 the point is at a certain position relative to the system of rectangular coordinates used. If Latitude and Longitude were used then the point would be defined '*relative to*' a different zero point of origin.

What I am trying to point out is that we are free to choose a system that suits our purpose, so it should not come as a surprise that an entity from somewhere else will use yet another system. Unfortunately there is an added complication with Mi's system. It does not involve numbers. Mi says that we rely too much on a number system to define a point's position instead of using the *properties* of the surroundings.

Mi gave a series of layers and intersecting lines which I have tried to represent in diagram 7. Looking at the diagram is almost like looking at a kind of stairway. The position of a point is in the upper layer, while a reference or 'ground' level is the bottom layer. Diagram 8 is another, more concrete, representation that was given, to indicate the different properties of each layer. In diagram 9 the layers have become 'twisted' except for the bottom one. In diagram 10 the layers become even more entwined and the whole thing forms some kind of 'sphere' around the point.

There is no explanation as to how the point's position is located. The first thing to remember is that from place to place, in a local region, the properties of that region vary slightly and it is this variation that Mi is able to detect.

However, we might be able to form a simplified version of this idea with the aid of a piece of paper. Write numbers on the paper in a random manner. Twist or fold the sheet in an anti-clockwise direction as shown in diagram 11. The numbers now become associated with other numbers in addition to the numbers written adjacently. This is basically what any object does when placed in the region – it links parts of that region not previously associated.

This leads us into redrawing diagrams 7 & 8. Diagram 12a shows a more realistic view of the layers, where the difference in the Grey color density represents the various zones actually merging at points where they meet. More than that, we are looking Mi's C.T. image and Mi calls this an 'operating zone'. Diagram 12b is really the next step.

These diagrams, as with previous ones, were originally in color and were more complex than those drawn here. However, there is a limit to the amount of understandable information that can be given in this way. Unfortunately, much of what was given was not understood, and could not be drawn.

Diagram 13a

Diagram 13b

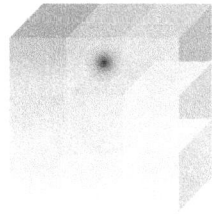

I have put the previous illustrations into a 3-D setting and Diagram 13a gives a more realistic touch to the idea of layers. However, this still does not go far enough, because in a given layer there will be variations maybe from left to right, or from top to bottom or both. Diagram 13b is an attempt to show this more complete view with a given point interacting with the surrounding regions.

Chapter 10 – Learning our ABCs'

The 'twisting' idea mentioned in the previous pages may be a mental process by Mi (assuming that the word mental applies), because if it is not, then this would imply that Mi life is able to manipulate, at least local regions in a physical way. I do not know which is correct as I have no evidence to support one view more than the other. While an actual physical manipulation is not impossible it does mean that if there are many Mi Life Forms and they are all manipulating in this way, then surely only chaos can result.

Diagram 14a

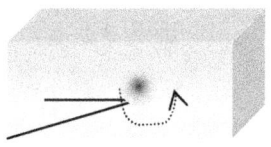

Diagram14b

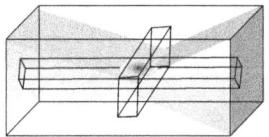

Diagrams 14a and 14b are intended to show the kind of 3-D twist that takes place, and the boxes in 14b are just the planes of the point. However, it seems to indicate that the kind of co-ordinate transformation that would be occurring is perhaps, more like that of Diagram 15 where the top becomes the bottom and left becomes right

Chapter 10 – Learning our ABCs'

Diagram 15

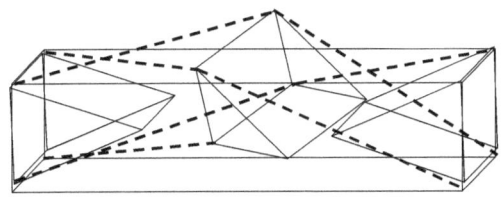

According to Mi, this is where *interconnecting lines* come into play. Mi says that these lines are a physical reality. They may be straight or curved according to the surroundings, which will determine any line's attributes.

Trying to comprehend these *interconnecting lines* was not easy or fully understood; perhaps the nearest analogy might that of an Interface.

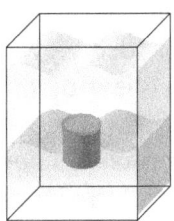

Diagram 16

I think the most common type of interface that people see is that of Oil and Water. Diagram 16 is a depiction of a piece of wood floating in water, with oil (or some other liquid lighter that water) floating on top of the water. All three components are quite visible, and here we have an example of liquid-solid interface, and liquid-liquid interface, and above the oil, a liquid-air interface.

Chapter 10 – Learning our ABCs'

Diagram 17

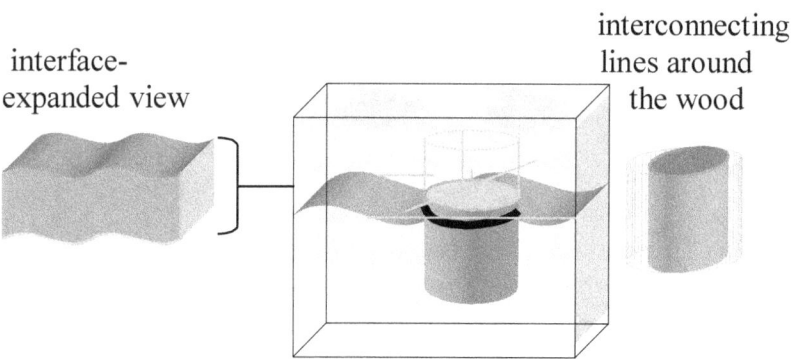

interface-
expanded view

interconnecting
lines around
the wood

Diagram 17 is an enlargement of Diagram 16 with lines drawn to show approximately where the interconnecting lines might be. The surfaces are shown as waves to indicate a non-static nature. On the LHS there is an expanded view of the liquid-liquid interface and on the RHS there is a view of the interconnecting lines around the piece of wood.

The interconnecting lines are the active components and the energy of these lines is not dependent on size but on the energy potential of the system involved. For example, liquids such as water and Chloroform would have more active interconnecting lines because there is more hydration taking place at the interface, than say that of water and pure oil. Another example would be if the piece of wood were radioactive.

It seems that what Mi Life is capable of doing, is being able to receive 'signals' from these interconnecting lines and make the appropriate analyses. If other signals were sent to the system, such as any form of Radar, these signals would modify the system, and thus on return to the source the modifying Radar signals would need to be 'analyzed out' before any conclusions could be made.

Some may think this is similar to what is usually portrayed by Bats, but I think it is closer to that of Sharks. Many biologists believe that the Shark is the most advanced streamlined fish in the

Chapter 10 – Learning our ABCs'

sea. The sea is much denser than the air and while sound moves faster, radio signals move fractionally slower than in air. When Sharks depend on sound and on their eyesight they make the mistake of eating all sorts of rubbish. However, it has been demonstrated that some species of Shark have very fine, accurate electromagnetic sensors that can guide the Shark to a particular point. At this time little is known about the mechanism, some thinking that the Sharks can 'think' about the destination, others believe it is pure instinct. [Another point about the Shark is that once it was assumed that a Shark would drown if it stopped moving, because of the lack of the essential fish component, the Swim Bladder. Thus Sharks could never rest. It has been seen, however, that some Sharks can go into a 'dormant' state for several hours, and survive without drowning. This illustrates our illogical reasoning that just because 'something' doesn't possess what other similar 'things' have then that 'something' cannot do what the other similar 'things' can do].

From what Mi informed previously, it is not unreasonable to assume that these interconnecting lines have a magnetic property. Perhaps Sharks and other animals can sense the interconnecting lines, where we have apparently lost the ability to do so, or have not developed it because of our dependence on sight.

Diagram 18a   Diagram 18b

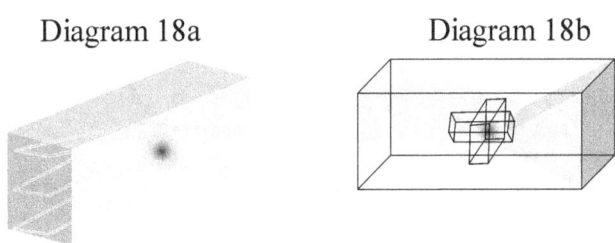

Chapter 10 – Learning our ABCs'

The foregoing diagram 18a, was given by Mi, and I have shown interconnecting 'planes' rather than lines. These planes are given a 3-D 'wrap around' in diagram 18b, which is similar to diagram 14.

The figure below, Diagram 19, shows the 'wrap around' effect of interconnecting lines as an enlargement of 18b. The long arrow from top rear left indicates movement to the lower front right, while the long arrow at lower front right indicates movement to top right rear. The smaller solid arrows indicate an outer movement while the dotted arrows indicate other movements. This is not the complete picture as interconnecting lines from other directions are also present.

Thus the point becomes completely enclosed with an already identified system, and therefore its location becomes known.

Diagram 19

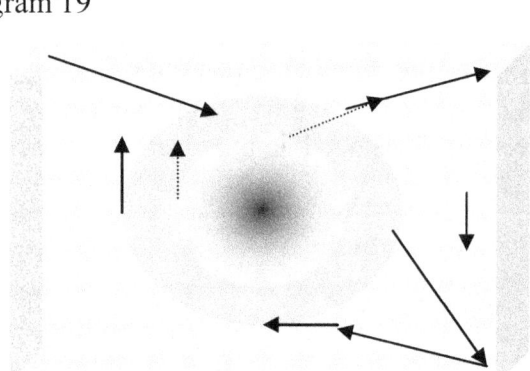

You will notice that *straight* lines rather than *curved* ones have been drawn. This was a surprise to me because it seemed that Mi preferred flat systems where I expected curved ones. Though there is no answer from Mi as to why this is, we will later revisit this question.

Chapter 10 – Learning our ABCs'

Mi pointed out that the above diagrams illustrate a process that is not normally used by Mi life and only used here in explanation. The analogy here is that when we are discussing a particular argument with one another, we don't explain or speak of every step we are making. If we did so we might spend more time noting every step than we did with the actual point of discussion. We simply speak our mind and explain only when asked to do so.

Three questions were now asked of Mi.

1. How can we Humans do this?
2. What if a point is in a region not already identified?
3. How does an unidentifiable region become identifiable?

Questions 2 & 3 were quickly discarded by Mi, and Mi asked:

'Where is this unidentified region? Is there such a place?'

As for question 1, Mi was quite definite, stating that Humans *already do it!*

Example 1

When watching T.V. I am asked by someone (equally familiar with the surroundings as I am) the whereabouts of a certain article. What is my usual form of answer? If I know the location then I merely state the location; if I don't know the location of the item I may state a location where I last saw the item. On the other hand I will rarely use numbered measurements because the item is enclosed within an identified system. (Note that I have used the term 'system' rather than 'area')

Example 2

Say I have left my car at some particular place because it has broken down. If I have left it at a known position in town, again I will use the location term because someone else's mind will immediately 'go' to that location. However, supposing I leave the car on a road where there are no obvious identifiable areas. What do I say? 'I have left the car by the tree with the broken branch'. No, I will more than likely use some system of measurement along such and such a road.

Chapter 10 – Learning our ABCs'

Example 3
Perhaps I hold a party and one of the guests, say, is the real party type. As this person enters people's faces light up as they go and greet the him/her. Or maybe at the other extreme the person is dismal, full of woe and usually bores people with stories of misfortune.

In examples 1 & 3, according to Mi:
People can identify with each other and the surroundings without the use of numbers.

We affect each other in many ways that we would find difficult to express in numbers, yet we are able, very often, to be quite precise. [Mi refers to ' love-ness' and 'hate-ness'].

Example 2 according to Mi:-
Shows that we have become lazy in not developing senses that have existed in our brains for a long time; that other animals do show a greater ability to recognize interconnecting lines and planes on a local level but do not have the capacity or opportunity to develop further. Human beings have both the capacity and opportunity.

The Mi entity distinguishes between Instinct, Operating Time Component and Apo-volintive recognition. 'Apovolintive' is a word that we have been unable to find. Human instinct, according to Mi, is the basic level where we react automatically to the interconnection but cannot differentiate the significance of the interconnection.

An analogy to this would be say, calling out to a friend in some busy street using their Christian name. My friend could turn their head, but so could several other people with the same name. I might narrow the field down a bit by using the other names of my friend.

Here we have examples of reacting instinctively to names, another point that we will visit later.

Mi declares that we are too dependent on numbers and sight. We have become 'lazy' and allowed our natural senses to become overruled by abstract ideas. Mi states that there are many examples where our natural abilities have been shown to be

Chapter 10 – Learning our ABCs'

superior to any abstract system, yet we continue to ignore them. We, states Mi, are very busy with calculating our relationship with our universe and neglect trying to realize our reaction with it.

Chapter 11 – End of the beginning

We consider ourselves as Carbon based life forms, and though there are other 'trace elements' involved, the main constituents are Hydrogen, Nitrogen and Oxygen, and it is Carbon that is the main carrier, or hub, for the others.

Just as we saw that the Atomic Number of Lawrencium was 103, that of Carbon is 6, Hydrogen is 1, Nitrogen is 7 and Oxygen is 8.

Water, H_2O, the most precious of all to us humans, has a Molecular Weight of 18. Plants use Carbon Dioxide, CO_2, to manufacture their constituents. Without plants we all know where *we* would be. The Molecular Weight for CO_2 is 44. The Atomic Weight of Carbon is 12, and it is from here that the word counts for 'Mi', 'twin' and 'Mira Ceti', as well as the factor Tridel itself, can be derived – a coincidence?

There is yet a more important coincidence. These days, the words Amino Acids and Proteins from Chemistry and Biology are well known. Amino Acids are the basic building blocks of Proteins and are linked together by what is called a *Peptide* Bond, and this bond has a single identity. It has the molecular structure:

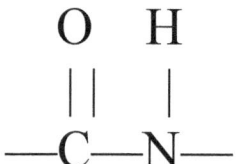

As you can see, there are only four elements involved in this all important bond and they are those that we have just been considering, Carbon, Hydrogen, Nitrogen and Oxygen. Is this also *just* a coincidence?

With regard to the science of Physics we look at a formula that is basically Kepler's third law, which states that the square of the period of a planet is proportional to the cube of its mean distance from the Sun. This is used, along with Gravitational and Mass / Radius figures, in a simple formula when calculating

Chapter 11 – End of the beginning

distances of satellites from the Earth: the Tridel factors can replace part of the formula. The result turns out to be different by about 0.006 of 1%. However, I do point out that the resulting difference for a small satellite orbiting the Earth with a period of 24 hours (the satellite being stationary relative to the Earth's surface – [geosynchronous]), is just over $1\frac{1}{2}$ miles in an average orbiting height of just over 26,460 miles.

However, the most important point for us here is that the standard expression for calculating this radius (height in this case) involves the Earth's average gravitational force. This can be equated to an expression using only Tridel. So we are definitely standing on a 'springboard' to more advanced topics.

Mi answered that Mi life was not human, yet the above is suggestive of some kind of biological link is it not? Another alternative may be that similar life forms may exist on other planets that have a relationship to Tridel. For example, the much publicized evidence for life existing, or at the very least having existed, on Mars may be reflected by comparison with its physical data to that of Earth. If we take the rotation periods to the nearest half hour we have Earth with 24 hours and Mars at 24.5 hours. Multiplying these by Tridel gives 88 and 89.83333...respectively. I am not suggesting that sub-multiples of Tridel (in this case 89.83333333333333333...= 88 + ½Tridel) is important because adding 1 to twin digit numbers will give similar results. However, what may be important is the *range*, perhaps something like 88 plus or minus $\frac{1}{2}$ Tridel, or 88 plus or minus Tridel, and that planets with rotation periods within these limits have water to support similar life forms. Once again, I am not suggesting that these are the only considerations to be taken into account, but it may be possible to construct a formula involving Tridel to represent Life, that is, Life as we know it.

This is all very well but what about the experience itself. What about Mi, if indeed that is the entity's real name? Was this name given to me so that we would eventually turn up these relationships? Where did Mi decide to start? Did Mi start with the constellation of Cetus, or did Mi start with the biological details of human kind? The names of the stars are just that, names given by

Chapter 11 – End of the beginning

some group of people, quite different from the group that gave the names to the Chemical elements, as in the case of Lawrencium.

Is Mi just 'a naughty little boy' who has disobeyed a rule about not interfering with Human Beings and is just 'playing'? Or has Mi sent a real signal of importance to us? How could Mi have known all these details?

Let us see if we can deduce some plausible hypothesis from the confusion.

I am intrigued by the way ancient and mythological figures turned up and why they should do so at all. Norman's introduction of Enki seems to have been most important, because the word count of 39 turns up repeatedly with further answers reminiscent of both Tridel and the gravitational constant.

Then there was the word 'trio' which was derived from the names of the Norse deities, in 'look hind trio'. The answer was a figure of 88 and 88 divided by Tridel equals 24. Or do we need to look somewhere between Enki and Thor because 'Enki' minus 'Thor' is equal 'Mi'!

We have looked at the 'coincidences', deduced certain properties and made some theories based on these deductions. We have taken a brief look at how a system might develop to make certain calculations without the necessity of numbers, although the system was somewhat awkward and clumsy. I hinted in the last chapter that we might be able to deduce something about Mi's whereabouts, but there has not really been any advance on this most crucial point.

It would seem that Mi had considerable difficulty in contacting me, and was only successful on what appeared to be the second attempt. There could, of course, have been other attempts, but I have only been aware of two. Why was it that there needed to be a move eastward from England? Certainly it would have brought me five thousand miles closer to the mysterious point in China, Mi, but 5000 miles in comparison to the Cosmos is not even noticeable. Perhaps the place, Mee (Mee is an old English name), on the Moon needs to be considered too and perhaps a certain angle of alignment between these and a third point. The 'crying' was heard in both places but perhaps 'fine tuning' was necessary.

Chapter 11 – End of the beginning

Apart from the image, Mi has not made a 'personal' appearance, unless we consider the mysterious Lady as connected to Mi. This connection seems unlikely though, since if, as she 'told' me in one of those very vivid dreams, I would be with her after I die, why did she not mention something about Mi also? Mi was also definite in a negative response towards questions of gender, and made it obvious that no indication was going to be given. So again this might suggest that the two experiences are unrelated. In this way, who or whatever the mysterious lady is, she has the advantage over Mi in being able to present herself. Or perhaps she is much 'closer' to me than Mi is.

So a theory from the above confusion might run like this. Mi would have to make sure that Mi's 'homework' was quite thorough, so that any messages could be communicated before the end of a certain period. It is then reasonable to assume that the message, along with the mathematical implications, would contain items about our fundamental sciences of Chemistry and Physics, and thus work out in the system to derive Tridel. However, there is a bit of a gap – why involve Mira Ceti? If, as I suggested earlier, Mira Ceti was a fundamental ingredient, then surely its position would have been considered by Mi similar to the position of Lawrencium being 103, was important. So is there another topic we need to consider?

What we haven't yet done is to look at the sky.

The next point is too important to just skip over and must be considered in detail. I constructed a diagram (not shown here) to represent the portion of a star map shown on the page 127. Using the diagram I calculated the area of various segments (rectangular and triangular) of interest and the main result is given below. During my computations I derived a figure of 1068 and another figure very close to it by considering the two central components, Mira Ceti and Lawrencium. Two other results, 180 and 10740, were similarly derived. Let us consider the figure 1068 first.

If you look up the New General Catalogue, always referred to as NGC, you will find NGC 1068, which just happens to be in the constellation of Cetus. NGC 1068 has another name, M77, which means it was the seventy seventh object in the Messier

Chapter 11 – End of the beginning

catalogue. So we have yet another 'twin'. M77 is a Seyfert galaxy and has been estimated to be 18.4 mega Parsec (1Parsec = 3.26 light years), that is, 59.984 million light years distant from us. M77 is very close to the Celestial equator and is located on the upper right on the star map.

Now, dividing 10740 by the other figure obtained, 180, we get 59.666666667 which when divided by 3.26 = 18.3. This is close to the figure of 18.4 just mentioned. So from Lawrencium 119+103 and Mira Ceti 41+37 we have arrived at a complete set of figures, 1068, 180 and 10740 from which is derived information about M77.

Looking towards the center of the star map, you can see χ Ceti and just below is ζ Ceti. χ, Chi is the 22nd letter of the Greek alphabet while ζ, Zeta, is the 6th letter of the Greek alphabet. Greek letters were used to number the stars until it became obvious that the number of letters was not sufficient for naming stars within constellations. One should be mindful that we are looking below the celestial equator, so that χ Ceti is slightly more southerly than ζ Ceti, or to put it another way, 6 over 22 the inverse of Tridel!. Mira Ceti can be located further to the right and 66 lower left of Mira.

It turns out that the total area of interest is 165 square degrees and the objects mentioned above are all in the left half. The area of the containing triangle is therefore 82.5 square degrees. Contained in this triangular area, using Mira Ceti as the corner of smaller rectangle connecting with the sides of the main total area, is a resulting rectangular area is 22.5 square degrees. Divide 82.5 by 22.5 and the answer is exactly Tridel. Is Mi's whereabouts or Mi's time / dimensional connection somewhere here? The next chapter is all-important in trying to answer this question.

You may be wondering about the validity of the claim that the stars χ Ceti and ζ Ceti may represent Tridel, since their positions would indicate the *inverse* of Tridel. If you add Tridel to Norman's full name count the result is 377.666666667. Now multiply this by 6 and then divide by 22 and the answer is...103, equal to Lawrencium's Atomic number. Originally Lawrencium was deduced from my name, but had I formulated Tridel first I might have deduced Lawrencium from Norman's name.

Chapter 11 – End of the beginning

As you can see below, the two stars that support my theory about Tridel *appear*, to the eye, to be in close proximity in the constellation of the Sea Monster. Norman's introduction of Enki, who among other things, was the 'God of water', could have referred to some other constellation (such as Aquarius or Eridanus for example), so was I meant to introduce Mira Ceti to specifically identify the constellation of Cetus?

I therefore have to conclude that the above not only confirms my earlier derivations of Tridel, but places Tridel in a very strong position regarding the experience as a whole.

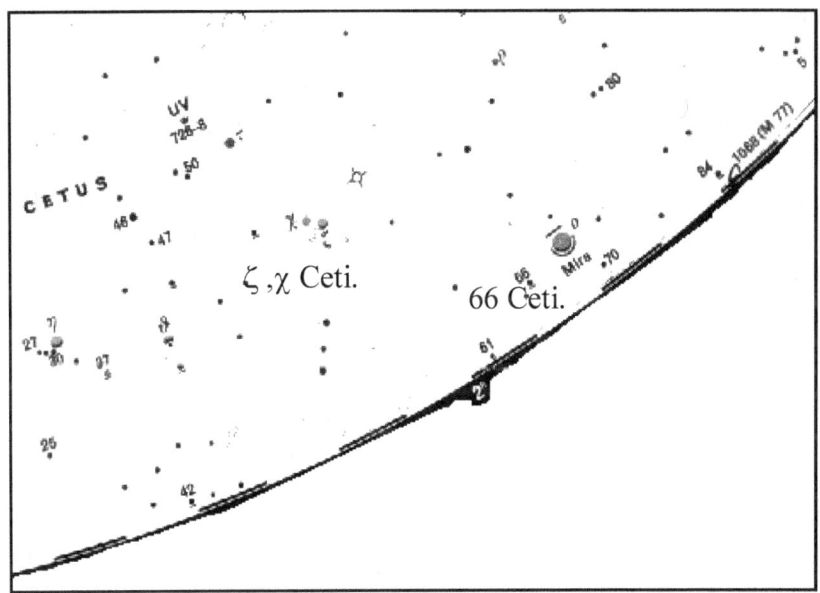

Chapter 12 – Chimes of Time

There are two reasons why I wanted to leave Mi ideas about Time until now. Firstly, Time as we currently understand it, is a difficult enough concept to examine as it is (although we do take it very much for granted), let alone try to understand it from a different standpoint. Secondly, I had hoped that previous chapters might show some technique on how to visualize Mi Time. It would seem that I have failed. We will have been, up to this point, just as much in the dark as we were before with regard to Mi's ideas. Having said that, the preceding work and that of current study, suggests that Mi had everything worked and mapped out. If this is the case then surely the key to unlocking the door to Mi's ideas is here in our possession, somewhere.

I was sure that the information was staring me in the face, yet I was unable to fathom a formula, or expression, which might fit the four categories of Time as perceived by Mi. Now two years after the experience, in the early part of 2002, I was beginning to think that I had gone as far as I could, and that I would have to concentrate, perhaps, on MI's ideas about the Magnetic Time field.

Then something quite incredible happened to Norman at his home, though I chose not to consider it until a couple of months later. Incredible because………Well, read Norman's own words about what happened.

***

The incidents concern chimes from my doorbell – or, to be more precise, apparently emanating from a source close to and from the 'remote' speaker in our lounge. The first of these occurred on Sunday 3rd March 2002, after which I sent the following e-mail to Larry: -

"....At 12.42GMT I was coming into the lounge from the kitchen when the doorbell chimed – only it wasn't the doorbell! About two months ago we fitted a new doorbell with a 'remote' speaker that you can take from room to room – but we usually leave it on the music centre in the lounge by the door to the passage, where it was today and most days. This doorbell has a two-tone chime – 'ding-dong – (two notes). However, what we heard today was TWO sets of FOUR chimes, much deeper and louder than is normal (Think of

Chapter 12 – Chimes of Time

Big Ben striking the half-hour and you won't be far out!). My wife got up and went to the door – which is some 20-25 yards up the drive from the gate. I followed her. No-one was at or anywhere near the door in any case and the gates were shut."

"....No neighbours were around. We thought of an ice-cream van, but none was in the vicinity and no engine noise had been heard at the time anyway. Also, I fancy an ice-cream van's chimes would have gone on longer. Electrical equipment in that part of the lounge consists of the doorbell 'speaker': a music centre (both already referred to) and a TV and Video Recorder. The recorder was switched off, though 'on' at the power point. I'd switched on the TV at 12.30 to watch the Australian Grand Prix – replayed by ITV from the night before: (earlier in the day, actually, because it had been shown 'live' around 2am), but I'd gone out to the kitchen to get something before the race actually began. The music centre was switched off at the power point."

"....To my mind, the source of the chimes seemed not actually to be the 'speaker', but to be two or three feet above and away from the music centre, this being next to the speaker."

"...O.K. That was odd enough, but at 1.12pm. (13.12), precisely half-an-hour later, the same thing happened. I was sitting in an armchair by the window: my wife was in an armchair by the far wall. It's a very large lounge, and she would have been eighteen to twenty feet from the sound, and I'd have been eight to ten feet (always assuming that my estimate of source – which seemed to be precisely as before) is correct."

"...I then thought that since it seemed the second chimes had occurred precisely half-an-hour after the first, that they could well recur again, and at 1.40pm (13.40), took up a position underneath where I thought the sound had come from, this being about an arm's length from the doorbell speaker, which I proposed to grab hold of and move if the chimes recurred, to see what the result, if any, would be. It seemed to me that the only possible piece of

Chapter 12 – Chimes of Time

equipment had to be the speaker – which, being a mobile operated by a battery-powered beam from the doorbell, I thought just possibly might have picked up emanations from a neighbour's doorbell or some other electrical equipment – though it would have had to be a pretty strong source, for the chimes were very loud, louder than the doorbell itself, which, even with four batteries, won't activate the speaker from a distance greater than 60ft."

"…However, no further chimes. I'm wondering, though, if they might recur at the same time early tomorrow morning, or perhaps precisely 24 hours later…."

Saturday 4th. May 2002

Well, they didn't recur 24 hours later. I made all the obvious checks – including asking the makers whether the speaker should actually be *able* to emit the eight notes – was it within its 'remit' to do this? According to them, it was, so far as they were aware, not possible. The incident had slipped to the back of my mind when, at two minutes past six (18.02) on May 4th. they occurred again. The conditions were precisely as before, but this time there was no 'follow-up' half-an-hour later. Interestingly, about three hours previously there had been an 'ordinary' ring at the door without anyone apparently present. ('Ordinary' being two notes, the chimes at 6.02pm again having eight notes – six of which the speaker shouldn't know about). This time, my wife and I were sitting in armchairs about fifteen feet apart. At precisely two minutes past ten (22.02) we were again treated to a repeat performance, hearing them from precisely the same positions. As I put in a further e-mail to Larry a day later, 'The 'ordinary' chime of the bell is 'ding-dong' – high note/lower note. The 'alien' chimes consisted of eight notes in two sets of four in a different cadence to the 'ordinary', the two sets being different to each other. Nothing further till……..

Sunday 8th. December 2002

Chapter 12 – Chimes of Time

One set of four chimes was heard at 10.45am. GMT when we were both in different rooms to the speaker and to each other. My wife was in the kitchen, outside which is the bellpush. I was in a bedroom. There was no-one at or anywhere near the door.

Sunday, 2nd. February 2003

This occurred at 8.30pm. (20.30GMT). This time they again reverted to eight notes (as far as one could tell, the same eight notes). Again no one around anywhere at all. On this occasion there was deep snow all around and there were no footprints at all, other than my own, the whole 50-60 feet to the gate! The weather also excluded the 'ice-cream van' hypothesis.

Finally – to the time of writing, (December 2003), they occurred again on Saturday 3rd. May, 2003, when I sent the following e-mail to Larry: -

"...Thought you might like to know that the chimes recurred today about half-an-hour ago (Saturday, May 3rd. 2003 –03.05.03 at 3.54pm. BST -15.54)

Eight notes – two sets of four, separated by a second's pause, as on the half-hour.

Seating arrangements precisely as before – my wife reading a newspaper and me doing a crossword. Position of speaker as previously.

My wife went to the door but no-one was there. Actually, it is now impossible for anyone to ring the bell in any case, since about ten days before we went to the USA I found there was no bellpush! This had been affixed to a square of wood by superglue. In turn this square was screwed in with rawlplugs to the brickwork. The square of wood remains, but the bellpush is, as I say, no longer there. Nor, when I noticed the absence of the bellpush about a month ago, was it to be found on the path below.

Chapter 12 – Chimes of Time

Am tempted to carry the speaker around with me or in the car. Could raise some interest if it recurred whilst shopping or having my hair cut!

Best   Norman PS.
As I type this, it's just done it again at 3.18pm. (15.18BST) and at 3.21pm. (15.21BST). Me at the computer both times. My wife in the garden at 15.18 and in the kitchen at 15.21. On the last occasion got to the speaker in time to hear the last chimes – definitely they come from the speaker itself, not anywhere else –N.."

Precisely the same thing occurred again at 8.45pm (20.45) and 8.52pm (20.52) the same night. Following these two occurrences, Larry suggested I have a bell handy and ring it after they occur. Well, we do have a cowbell hanging in the hall but, to date, there has been no repeat of the chimes, so no occasion to use it.

There, for the moment the matter rests. The problem, of course, is that it's impossible to predict when they're going to recur, and they're over so quickly that, by the time one has reached the apparent point of origin, they've finished. By the same token it's also impossible to record them! I'm hesitant, even now, definitely to ascribe them to a 'non-material' source such as MI, even though, from Larry's deductions, it would so appear. The one common fact is, perhaps, that they were all heard at the weekend – on a Saturday or Sunday, which MIGHT just have a significance should someone around, normally at work during the week be indulging in some form of electronic experimentation. However, I could find no neighbour who would admit to such, and, as the bungalows around are quite widely spaced, this would mean that only three of them could be the source anyway.

One last point – followed by a table. I originally thought that we heard four sets of chimes on the first occasion, but for some reason, by the time I e-mailed Larry, began to doubt this – why, I don't know, and was then more inclined to there having

Chapter 12 – Chimes of Time

been only two sets – the 'half-hour' rather than the 'hour'. However, in response to the e-mail from Larry where he refers to following the 'table' – asking if I could identify the notes, I included my interpretation of all four sets, taking them as having had precisely the same cadence as the 'Big Ben' chimes since this is how they came over to me. It is odd that I have this dichotomy of memory for that first occasion – my wife could not be sure either. Memory can be a tricky thing! For this reason I would not personally be absolutely sure that numerological possibilities and sequences derived from their notes must of necessity be completely accurate, though I have to agree that all forms of 'normal' explanation for the chimes themselves seem to have been exhausted. 'MI' would certainly appear to be the most likely possibility, therefore.

Table of dates for Chimes

Sunday 3rd. March 2002 12.42.GMT Two/Four(?) sets of four chimes
                              13.12. GMT   Ditto
Saturday 4th. May 2002 18.02. BST Two sets of four chimes
                              22.02. BST   Ditto
Sunday 8th. December 2002 10.45 GMT One set of four chimes
Sunday 2nd. February 2003   20.30 GM Two sets of four chimes
Saturday 3rd. May 2003 15.54 BST   Two sets of four chimes
                              20.45 BST   Ditto

Aside from 'weekends' being prominent, one thing perhaps of note from the table is that all dates were quite early in the month and, indeed, two of them were within one day of each other, but in different years (May 4th.2002 and May 3rd. 2003 respectively.)

***

In September I wrote for details on the notes played by the chimes, and on receiving this information from Norman I replied with the following.

Chapter 12 – Chimes of Time

21-9-2002

"Dear Norman, thank you for the e-mail concerning your chimes. What I am doing is that I am only taking notice of your first alternatives. That is CGAD DEFD CGAD DEFD (or CBAD), and BFGC CDEC BFGC CDEC (or BAGC). I will not try to evaluate the other alternatives, because I will probably find at least one that fits what I am looking for. What I am saying is that I will consider your first impressions as being closer to the truth, as it were. Just to consider these is going to take some considerable time. At this time, based upon the first four I have a small indication that Mi may be referred to, as well as Lawrence and Oliver. I will let you know more once I have had the chance to study them in more detail.

All the best

Larry"

The main reason that I would consider only the first alternative is that I know of Norman's attitude for exactness. My determination to search for the truth is well matched by Norman's attitude for exactness, which is probably why we made a good 'team' back when I was NIC in BUFORA. Indeed, I now wonder why Norman and I never headed our own organization for researching strange phenomena, but 'there you go', it wasn't to be, which is probably why we are both where we are now.

The first thing I did with Norman's information was to arrange two sets in a Modulo Arithmetic* pattern. In this case, the sequence is 1, 2, 3 and then repeating. i.e. A = 1, B = 2, C = 3, D = 1, G = 1. The two sets are also numbered according to the musical scale A to G, that is 1 to 7.

---

*

Modulo Arithmetic is simply 'circular' arithmetic and you are using it when you look at an analogue watch or a clock. If the time piece has numerals one to twelve this is Modulo 12 because once the time reaches 12 o'clock the cycle starts again.

Chapter 12 – Chimes of Time

Set 1	CGAD	=	3111	Set 2	BFGC	=	2313
	DEFD	=	1231		CDEC	=	3123
	CGAD	=	3111		BFGC	=	2313
	DEFD	=	1211		CDEC	=	3123

$$\text{Diagonal} = (3211 = \text{CBAD}) \qquad (2113 = \text{BAGC})$$

Set 1	CGAD	=	3714	Set 2	BFGC	=	2673
	DEFD	=	4564		CDEC	=	3453
	CGAD	=	3714		BFGC	=	2673
	DEFD	=	4564		CDEC	=	3453

The first coincidence to note is that there were two sets of four, which seemed to contain a repeat. This, to me, had the feel of the 'twin' idea. They might have some similarity with the earlier 8×3 word matrix but, however, I found no similarities.

The next coincidence is that the Leading Diagonal of each of the corresponding number sets was actually identical to Norman's other two possible alternatives (in brackets). I find it amazing that such a thing happened.

The following coincidence was mathematical but in short, both had the calculated value of zero. This would seem to confirm that Norman had chosen correctly because some mathematical expressions equal to zero are important as 'stationary points'.

However, this may have been an indication that these two arrays, by themselves, have zero meaning. So with this in mind I then proceeded to use features from previous analysis.

The number 1880, had appeared in other computations in previous months, connected to an ellipsoid that I had computed. Since, in the chimes, the first two series are repeated in both sets I used just the first two series of the first set. I chose to treat the figures as numbers and the answer to a sum is 1880 – well, what a coincidence, and we've only just started.

Now, since I considered that by themselves the two sets of four might not yield much, I multiplied them together. The result is another set of four rows and each row has a total of 56. It just

Chapter 12 – Chimes of Time

happens to be the case that when the whole numbers of the computed ellipsoids, and an associated rectangle, are added sequentially (as in the earlier chapter on names), the answer is 56. Another coincidence?

This was only the tip of an iceberg, so to speak, because many more numerical coincidences occur. For example it turns out that by using Norman's figures for his chimes I can deduce Norman's 'twin' introduction and using Tridel I can identify with Mira Ceti and Lawrencium.

Now, the important question; assuming it *was* the entity Mi who was responsible for the chimes experience, why would Mi do something that would give results that we had already obtained from previous material? There are several possibilities but the one that seems most logical to me (in the present context) was that in deriving the above numbers we would instantly recognize them. Might such numbers be Mi's *signature*?

One might suggest that if Mi wanted to send a signature why didn't Mi just the word value of 22?

It so happens that 22 is there in the first series of the first set, 3111. The sequential value for this is 6 and $6 \times$ Tridel = 22. Mi realizing that I would use the new factor. However, if we take 22 as being a twin of 2's we can also find 22 in the second set. By totaling and then use the scale A to G, that is 1 to 7, then two 9's would be a return to the second key of two B's. Since 'b' is the second note we have two 2's.*

However, the overriding question must be, why contact Norman at all? What is the point of repeating information that we have already derived? Well I suppose one might suggest that it was through a musical interpretation of mi = mira that instigated study in this direction anyway and I don't have any musical chimes to play around with.

I thought that maybe Mi might give some information that we do NOT have yet, OR provide another way of determining future values, OR maybe Mi had already given the information, and I had failed to see it.

One problem that I had failed to resolve previously was about Enki, who has proved important, and which was Norman's

Chapter 12 – Chimes of Time

introduction. The only 'god' that I could associate with was Odin with whom I had a conversation in a dream. The word values for Enki and Odin added together equal 81, which is the same value as Norman's surname and my first name, but I was never able to equate Enki with Odin. For one thing Odin was a 'chief god' while Enki was the son of a 'chief god'. In the 8×3 matrix system (page66/67) Odin is 3132 and Enki would be 2223. By adding each to its 'mirror' image both results are the same, 5445.* The chime that put me on to this in the first place was the first series of the second set, 2313. So with the introduction of the chimes I had solved a nagging irritation.

Having satisfied myself that Norman had received a 'visit' from Mi, I wondered whether or not I could take things a stage further. The one important piece of information from Mi was about the categories of Time. I had spent much time on this problem with very little to show for it. Was there an answer in the chimes? I returned to considering the two sets and their values.

By finding the number of *occurrences* of each letter in Set 1 and those in Set 2, then subtracting Set 2 from Set 1 we end up with 4 letters. With the result I formed an equation where the coefficients (the numbers preceding each letter) are balanced to equal zero, $2a-2b-4c+4d$.* Another mathematical value also equals zero. Four Mi Time categories and four letters from the chimes and it was at this point where it occurred to me that there was a vague similarity between these and the equations I had asked Mi to solve (see previous chapter). Were we being presented with a similar situation to that which I presented to Mi?

The question remains that if $2a-2b-4c+4d$ (hereafter the 'Chimes expression') is applicable to Mi's Time idea, what are the values of a, b, c, and d? If I was simply to use trial and error, it might take a long, long time to find an answer, using all the accumulated figures. One way to shorten the search would be to look at the previously derived numbers and see if any of them had a relationship that gave a Linear Law when plotted on a graph.

I want to regress a little at this point, back to Norman's 'time table'. There are a couple of observations to be made about the dates. Firstly, there were *three* dates in the year 2002, and the

Chapter 12 – Chimes of Time

first date was the *third* day of the *third* month. Secondly, the *third* date, December 8th, was my birthday. Then there are a total of eight occasions when the chimes were heard. However, a third '8' is not apparent. Even so we still seem to be in the '3's' and '8's' domain and I wondered if there was an '8×3' somewhere? Just by coincidence the answer is yes, and Tridel is also included.

Next is the observation that the year 2002 is composed of mirror images. The number 2002 is exactly devisable by Tridel and the answer is exactly *three* times my name count.

So an interpretation of these figures might be that Norman was due to hear the Chimes on my birthday since the year number has a connection with my name count and the new factor, Tridel. However, this then poses two important questions. One is that if the year number has a connection to me why did I not experience something relevant during that year? The second is opposite to the first – why is there an absence of Norman's name count in the figures?

This has all the markings similar to those I experienced before, when I first heard the crying. Norman didn't have an entity experience but he heard something (although here Norman's wife also heard the Chimes). Now, since I have suggested a type reverse situation can our name counts provide any clues?

Computations suggest that this may be so, and that certain pursuits suggest a figure of 99 which when divided by Tridel equals 27, 3 above Mi's 24.

The regression now finished it is back to the Chimes

Ideally, I would be searching for four numbers which might have differences of one and two, similar to the derived Chimes expression. However, for the sake of thoroughness I ought to use all the numbers that have been used in previous chapters. For example the number 181 was used in the calculation of an ellipse (bottom of page 135) and is equal to the count for Mira Ceti and Lawrencium's Atomic number, 103. Proceeding in this way I tried to pair numbers together and the result was a list of twenty four pairs. From here, after some rearrangement, I produced quadruplets from those and termed them 'tetrads'. Once this was done many numerical coincidences were found. For example, only 24 tetrads

Chapter 12 – Chimes of Time

could be produced. All satisfied the expression from the Chimes expression, with the lowest member representing 'a' and 'd' the highest. I realized that all of these would have some properties in their favor, so I proceeded to check the twenty-four tetrads. Some tetrads had more in common with previous results than others, which led me to think that one or two of them might be 'indicators' of some kind.

It is possible, of course, and you may think it obvious, that *all* twenty-four tetrads are intended for use in some way. While I would agree with this, I don't think that all of the problems I have in mind will be solved by using all of the tetrads. Some problems require some unique values. In addition to this why would some tetrads stand out more than others?

I therefore had what seemed a very long job in front of me and I somehow felt that there was a criterion I should be using. What it was did not come to me easily, but when I did realize it, because of its simplicity, I wondered why I had not thought of it before. There were four alphabet letters in the Chimes expression and we consider that we exist in a four dimensional space-time continuum. In scientific books three of those dimensions are almost always referred to as X, Y and Z that is length, breadth and width. I finally arrived at a conclusion that two of these tetrads were more important than the others.

I was now in a position, perhaps, to try to evaluate Mi's four Time zones.

Mi seems to have made no suggestion that Time, as Mi views it, is either a scalar or vector quantity and the entity must have considered that I should reason this out for myself. With perhaps some overlapping 'grey areas', this seems to be fairly straightforward.

Both 'past time' and 'present time' were considered (by Mi) to be active time zones and thereby having gained a defined energy and direction. Thus we can conclude that these two must be at least partly, if not wholly, 'vectored'. The 'future time', being passive, probably contains more scalar properties. The difference between this and 'unused time' may be to do with deterministic physics, and 'future time' may be a direct selected potential vector

Chapter 12 – Chimes of Time

source. 'Unused time' would then be unselected and 'outside' all of these and could, theoretically, remain unused forever.

I must admit there may be some people who would consider quite the reverse. That is, the past may consist of the accumulated 'frozen' images of the many present times. Thus it would be unmoving and though possessing energy would have no direction. However, I don't think this arrangement fits in with Mi's ideas, or those of the Chimes expression and tetrad numbers. So for the time being I will proceed on the assumptions made earlier.

If 'unused time' is not yet a vector source and might be considered as an 'ocean' of 'spare-time' then it will remain internally as a scalar quantity and perhaps the other time categories exist with their boundaries defined differently to this. Indeed, since theoretically, all Time must have been unused in the first place, then we might expect 'unused time' to be larger quantity of the four.

Ah, then because 'd' in the Chimes expression is the larger of the four then this represents 'unused time'. Well...no. Unless there is something *outside* of 'unused time' that is providing more 'unused time' then we have to look for a quantity that remains as 1, with or without the other three. In other words, 'unused time' is being changed into the others, but the whole remains the same; alternatively, if the others are converted back into the original form (the 'without' part) then the whole still remains.

Certain results with regard to Chimes expression seem to give conflicting ideas, but then I realized the Chimes expression had more than one use. Indeed, it has proved to be so useful in several areas that I doubt that I would have found certain answers without it.

For example, how many times have you calculated how much money you will have for spending on holiday? ' I have 'a' pounds on the first Monday, and I need to spend 'b' pounds for bills this month, and I get 'c' pounds at the end of the month, leaving 'd' pounds for holiday next month.' You could use the same formula for calculating a weekly, fortnightly, or even yearly expenditure, so it should come as no surprise that I have found yet another, third, use for the expression when looking at Mi's ideas.

Chapter 12 – Chimes of Time

The Chimes expression at first sight seems to be simplicity itself, and I am sure that you and I would be very pleased to have the final answer to it all right here. This chapter being probably the most arduous one so far, you could heave a sigh of relief, and maybe be free at last to form your own opinion.

Unfortunately this is not case and the Chimes expression is deceiving; where previously I have used elementary procedures, further ideas associated with the Chimes expression become decidedly more complicated. This, in itself does not cause any great difficulty, but I repeat – I am not a Mathematician and therefore it takes me longer to work things out.

The Chimes expression is deceiving because the simple sum does not provide us with any real information about how the four different Time categories, if that is what it represents, interact with our three dimensional universe. Indeed, it is considered we already exist in a four-dimensional space-time continuum. If we are to break this down further with Time having four separate yet interactive parts, then we would expect any calculations to be at least, more extensive. (If the Chimes expression is used in a similar way to that of 'Event Space' in Einstein's theory of Special Relativity, all the tetrads display 'Spacelike' results.).

However, you may be wondering about my idea concerning Mira Ceti and Lawrencium as being the central hub to all of these ramifications. You may ask that if they **are** indeed so significant can it be shown that they are important to the Chimes expression? In addition to this, what about the factors Tridel 1 and Tridel 2? The answer is yes in both cases and many numerical coincidences have been found. In fact so many were found I was beginning to wonder when it would stop. The figures would seem to confirm that Mira Ceti and Lawrencium are the central hub.

Though my computations may not be the only solution to the Chimes expression, the figures obtained are a signal that I am heading the right way. That the Chimes expression may be of use in more than one direction would indeed, match the multiplicity of ways from which various items in this book have been derived.

Some final remarks about the Chimes expression and the tetrads. Complete analysis may take considerable time since I think

Chapter 12 – Chimes of Time

that there should be a correspondence between the tetrads, the Chimes expression and Mi's ideas about Time. I have, indeed, found that the tetrads and the Chimes expression form a neat, compact presentation of four states, two of which are variable and two that are static, and therefore may very well be congruent with Mi's ideas.

Very well, you might say, but what does this all *mean*? For one thing it means that finally I am now in a position to redefine Time according to Mi's ideas.

Time is a multi-component field exclusive of Space and Matter, that is, in an abstract sense, without considerations of normal material in our universe, such as Planets, Galaxies etc. Time consists of four sub-component time fields. Notice that I say 'normal material'. I do not include such ideas as Black Holes and the like, since these need special considerations. In a practical sense, of course, the four time components must be considered along with our universe and **all** it contains. Indeed, Magnetism and Gravity are undoubtedly connected to at least two of the sub-components,

I am sure that the one question you would ask me, for example, would be:-

"Given the information from Mi, is Time Travel possible?"

If we are talking about MI's ideas on Time, the answer is YES. The answer lies within the concept of the mirror image and the Chimes expression. Mathematically, a 'mirror image' is produced through one or more *rotations*

A second question might be:

"Considering Time as we currently understand it, is Time Travel possible?"

What I have worked out so far suggests that our everyday concept of Time can only provide *part* of the answer. This includes

Chapter 12 – Chimes of Time

the Theory of Relativity. The reader may already be aware that the Theory of Special Relativity prohibits Time Travel, though with adjustments and some additional equations the situation changes.

Does the Chimes expression provide us with any possibilities regarding Mi's whereabouts? Using the equations of the second set given to Mi with the Chimes expression and name counts given herein, figures of about 2.4° and 2.4 days have been calculated. These form part of a theory in the next book, but only Mi would know if the figures represent anything close to the truth.

Chapter 12 – Chimes of Time

Bottom page 135

$3111 - 1231 = 1880$

Bottom page 136
$2313 = 9, 3123 = 9$
$2313 = 9 = 2$
$3123 = 9 = 2$

First paragraph page 137

$2223 + 3222 = 5445, 3132 + 2313 = 5445$
$2313 + 3132 = 5445$

Third paragraph page 137

$(2a + 0b + 2c + 6d + 2e + 2f + 2g) -$
$(0a + 2b + 6c + 2d + 2e + 2f + 2g) = 2a - 2b - 4c + 4d$

(Note that I have changed to lower case letters below for convenience)

Bottom page 138

$22 \ 24, 37 \ 39, 41 \ 45, 47 \ 0, 51 \ 57, 63 \ 66, 68 \ 69, 75 \ 77,$
$78 \ 81, 103 \ 119, 124 \ 144, 150 \ 0, 181 \ 182, \ 300 \ 374$

--------Epilogue-------

Sometimes, when the pencil has made deep impressions on my fingers and there is little to show for it, I begin to wonder. 'What I am doing and is it all really worth it?' After all there are many humanitarian problems today, shouldn't I be thinking about those? Then another idea, or approach, comes to mind and I pick up my pencil once more. Is it the challenge that drives me, or has Mi really affected me that much?

In October of 2005, my wife's sister and her English husband (also known to Norman) visited Thailand. Three or four times the gentleman came to chat with me, and we talked about general matters and watched a DVD or two. One occasion, however, sticks in my mind. He knew of my Mi experience and was very interested in the 'mysterious lady', but it was after he left that something struck me. I realized that I had talked about nothing but Mi for hours, so much so that I must have seemed almost (if not definitely) *obsessive* about the experience. I had to apologize to the chap the following day and he just smiled in acceptance. Be that as it may, I am *still* putting pencil marks on my fingers and with continuing study (that I call 'Mi Mathematics'), I have no idea when I will 'hang up' my pencil and stop. Maybe I won't. It has become my personal 'trek' and Mi probably realized that I would follow this path and unless Mi makes another appearance that is the way it will stay.

However, before I continue I think this is the right place to confront a couple of possible criticisms and I will begin with a fictitious example – that is fictitious because I don't know of such a case.

You have just been watching one of those midnight 'horror' movies, which was so 'horrible' that you have dozed off. You are woken up by the sound of a gunshot and you are looking down the barrel of a Colt '45 from one of those 1950's Cowboys. You reach out and quickly dispose of the apparent danger with a quick move using the remote control 'off' button. It seems that you dozed through one movie and woke up half way through another. Then you feel a tingling in your shoulder and a chill that runs down your spine, and standing up, you look behind. There in front of you is an apparition with a pitchfork in one hand and a pair of tree branch cutters in the other. There is an intolerable odor and you pinch your nose, then suddenly the apparition vanishes. It has left behind on the floor some kind of semitransparent gelatinous material. You telephone the Police (a very bold move indeed) and after a few questions (such as 'have you been drinking?') the semitransparent gelatinous material is placed in a container and taken away for examination.

A couple of days go by and then you receive an evening visit from a Police Sergeant and a chap dressed in plain clothes. The Sergeant doesn't look at all happy and he begins by cautioning you about wasting Police time. The other gentleman is a Forensic Chemist and he says, "As far as I can make out the sample from your floor is Orange Marmalade."

Little does anyone know, but you have had a visit from a disgruntled spirit of an Orange Grove worker who died by having the misfortune to drown in a vat of his own farm produce.

Any of the criticisms leveled at such an incident would really be based on a single idea – the search for truth. The Policeman could hardly be blamed for his conclusion since there is very little in your story that can be substantiated. He might have seen the same 'horror' movie as you did, and experienced the same effect, but I doubt whether that would improve your position. In the laboratory the Forensic Chemist may have not been aware of where his sample came from and his finding will be based on the results of certain tests. The Chemist cannot be blamed for his conclusion since it would be based on the Scientific Principle. It is this scientific principle that is the basis for our conventional advance in knowledge. Everyone depends on the fact that what happened yesterday can, under the same conditions, be reproduced on any other day. The ignition of your car's engine (or the Bus) or perhaps your 'pint at the local': the path to work or the taste of your cup of tea or coffee etc. Think of the chaos that would arise if the procedure had to be changed for each performance. In addition, these processes have to be independent, as far as possible, from the human beings performing them. A new car must work for everyone regardless of race, color or **language.** There, I have finally come to what could be a major criticism of this book.

--------Epilogue-------

Though there have been some other languages used, most of the deductions have been made using the English language, and this violates the scientific principle. My name count in English is different to that of the Thai language. Indeed, not only that, the pronunciation is different as well. In addition, for example, if Mi had contacted a Thai person, the sound 'mee' has two different translations. One means 'to have' and the other meaning is 'bear', the animal. The difference is not only in the way it is written but also in the tone of speech. Now, given Mi's apparent lack of expertise in spoken English, I would have grave doubts about Mi's ability to communicate in Thai properly, and thus I doubt whether a Thai person would be drawn to the same conclusions as I have. So on the face of it, scientific principle *is* violated.

The apparent violation is based on a misconception. My name, in any language, should be written down in my native tongue regardless of what language I'm using precisely for the reason stated above. Written in Thai script the pronunciation of my Christian name is not Law-ren-ce, but Loren and my surname is not 'Dale' but 'Del' or even 'Den'. It doesn't matter what the considerations amount to, my name in the Thai language is wrong. For example, if someone mispronounces your name you correct him or her using the correct pronunciation. Mind you, the same might be said of trying to translate a Thai name into English. So in this way names transcend the native language and become an object in their own right, and it stays that way until death. Our personal names do not violate the scientific principle.

As for appellations such as Mira Ceti, Lawrencium, Carbon and so on, I did point out earlier that these were selected and chosen during conferences to be standard names, independent of any language; the scientific principle is not violated. Well, I could continue to debate this but I would still reach the same conclusion so I think it is time to move on.

Norman's Chimes experience presented me with new 'coincidences' and just when I thought I was stumped, it opened another door for me and things fell into place as it were. Whether Norman's Chimes experience *was* due to the entity Mi or not, does not detract from its importance to me. On the other hand I certainly hope that it was Mi who precipitated the Chimes experience, because if it wasn't Mi then who…? You will later, understand why I believe Norman's Chimes experience was due to Mi.

My Mi experience led Norman and I into many avenues of investigation, some fruitful others not so. Our study of Enki was certainly surprising, and while Norman obtained information via the Internet, in February 2003 I purchased two books[†], one on Sumerian culture the other on Ancient Mesopotamian mythology.

Enki seems to have been the son of the god An and goddess Nammu. It appears it was at the behest of Nammu that Enki created Mankind and also a series of other deities (though Enki is not without fault here and, in my words, gets a 'clip round the ear' for his mistakes). The deities and demigods are supposed to serve the chief god, An. However, Enki is not without suffering; the female goddess Ninhursag bears eight plants from Enki, but Enki eats them. Ninhursag wounds Enki with a curse, causing eight afflictions, and then flees. However she is persuaded by others to return and she cures Enki's eight problems by giving birth to eight children, one for each affliction. [It should be noted that Enki is 'outranked' by other deities, one them being Ninhursag.]

So we may have here yet another coincidence with Mi's '…up to 24' and Enki; eight plants, eight afflictions and eight children. Could this have any connection with the '8's' mentioned in earlier chapters? Perhaps there is some connection with the 24 tetrads? However, it is difficult see what connection there would be to plants, wounds and children, if indeed that is what they were. It is common within historical notes that the translation is not one hundred percent certain, either due to missing pieces, or words having more than one meaning. For example, one author states that although some Sumerian engravings are quite clear and distinct, their meanings, however, remain a mystery.

One possible route might be to ascertain what species of plant was involved and where they were planted (at least one is a 'honey' plant). The way in which the 'curses' or wounds affected Enki's body, may be informative and though the affected parts were apparently all different, only five affected parts have been translated. Lastly, perhaps the names of the children might show a connection. I have to say that not all accounts about Enki are the same and there are variations. Most important, however, is that Enki is most definitely depicted as the Water God (and God of Wisdom), and his nearest counterpart from Greek mythology appears to be Poseidon. Enki is very definitely the god associated with the Me.

Having mentioned the Me, a word of apology here. I had previously used the spelling provided by the source and perhaps assumed its pronunciation was the same as in English. This was, however, incorrect and the correct pronunciation (as provided in the books) is the same as the English 'may'. However, I did not place any great importance, for this study, on the Me, so no other material herein is affected. Indeed, it may actually be relevant to us here.

'Me' in Sumerian would be pronounced the same as 'me' in the Latin (and present day Spanish for example) meaning 'to me'. The English 'me' sound does have its roots within similar European languages though the sound has changed, probably in Old English times. Whether there is a possible connection here or not will require further study. (See below).

You may remember that Norman and I failed to find a 'goddess of the sea', Egyptian or otherwise for the name of my (new) meditation guide. It so happens that in Sumerian mythology it is the goddess Nammu, mentioned above, who was the 'primeval sea' from which everything else began. However, up to the time of writing, I have not been able to find any picture or depiction of this ultimate deity.

The ancient Sumerian language (Cuneiform), developed and evolved, and it seems that Philologists have found that the entire script (excluding their number system) is arranged into eight columns and eighteen rows. We have another 'eight' coincidence and of course '18' is the mirror image of '81'; multiplying eight by eighteen equals 144 which is perhaps more important because 144 has occurred frequently herein. While there are 90° rotations of some of the script figures, I can find no mirror images, but figure number 84 of the script is composed of just two vertical parallel lines.

--------Epilogue-------

Norman's name-count and mine seem to be 'transformed' by 39. Consider our first and last names counts then take away from this 4 times 'Enki'. The answer is 103. This might represent 'Lawrence Dale' or the atomic number of Lawrencium. "Oh but…" you might argue, "this is just subtracting Norman's name from the addition. Of course you will end up with 103!" In reply, I would simply say it isn't my fault that the word count for "Norman Oliver' just happens to equate with a multiple of the count for 'Enki'. I agree that multiples of other word counts would achieve the same result, but then these 'other word counts' did not present themselves during our study

Enki had yet a third name (with threes and thirds ranking important herein, he would have, wouldn't he!) – Nudimmud. By simply adding all three name counts together the answer is…144 [I should have known!]; this means that there is a direct link to the counts of Lawrencium (plus its Atomic number) and Mira Ceti because 144 is the *difference* between 222 and 78.

Another interesting point is that 144 divided by Tridel equals the original name count, 39, plus $1/\text{Tridel}$. So, we end up on some kind of merry-go-round of coincidences. The total script of the ancient Sumerian language equates with the three names of one of Sumer's major deities which in turn equates with the 'glue number' (of the 'reaction chamber') also involving the principal players Mira and Lawrencium. This characteristic of the count for Enki clearly unites the word counts for Enki and Mi with Tridel.

Apparently the eyes were extremely important in Sumerian culture, and indeed achieved a holy status. In many of their art forms and drawings depicting Gods, People and Animals, the eyes became the most prominent feature and in some cases took up a major part of the area of the head. In some so called 'eye idols' the eyes seem to be the entire head of the figure. Although there were no examples given in the books, it was said that some of these idols possessed four eyes. Could this have a possible link with the image of Mi having twin pupils? I think not because there is no way of knowing how many of the idols existed. However, there is yet a more important reason why I think not. None of the Gods of the Sumer religion had more than two eyes, but Enki had a loyal 'messenger', who seems to have had the status of a personal aide. His name was Isimud (the letter 'i' in Sumerian has the 'ee' sound) and Isimud is the only deity which had…two faces on one head. This therefore means that Isimud would have had two sets of eyes. Now, remembering mirror image numbers let's do the same with this name:-

i s i m u d
d u m i s i

Just looking at the central portion you can see the term 'mi' is placed exactly below its reversed mirror image. You will also notice that in this construction there are four occurrences of the letter 'i' which, when spoken in English, could sound like 'four eyes'. The obvious question is – does the entity Mi have some relationship with the myths concerning Enki and Isimud? There is also what might be a mythological link to the star Mira. In the Sumer astronomical system there was a constellation called Iku and this seems to have a connection with Enki. The count for Iku is 41. Having said that, another (American) source gives the name as 'Ikuu' and this relates to the present day Constellation of Pegasus. The most important point is that when replacing *a*, *b* , *c* and *d* of the Chimes expression with m, i, i, and m respectively, the sum is 24 – Mi's '…to twenty four…' perhaps ?

A thought about the pronunciation of the Sumerian word, 'me'. I wondered if there might be connection with our month of 'May' and the pronunciation of the word 'me'.

'May' has a word count equal to 'Enki'…well, well.
In a non leap year:
24th of May = <u>144</u>th day
and in a leap year 366 minus 144 equals the
count for 'Lawrencium' plus its Atomic number

So in conclusion to this historical diversion, it would seem that Mi knew something of Sumerian culture, but whether these coincidences can be further connected to the Latin language (i.e.

Mira), remains to be seen. Enki was originally introduced herein by Norman, and I have become convinced that Mi thought of Norman as being very important. Norman, however, has his own ideas about this.

The study of mirror image numbers gives some interesting results, and no less than incredible coincidences on one or two occasions, though not necessarily connected with Mi. The major 'characters' all display an amazing array of coincidences, and I am forced to conclude there exist relevant connections between Enki, Lawrencium, Mira, Norman, myself and Tridel.

The twenty-four tetrads certainly deserve some further observations. The fact that I derived them at all and then later used them with the 'Chimes' expression, which was derived from Norman's 'Chimes experiences', must rank as another incredible coincidence. However, I have to say that in their numerosity there is a certain misleading nature that might result in a fate similar to that of the Oozelum Bird. Nevertheless, certain approaches have proved useful, and I will mention one here.

The tetrads, Chimes expression and the simultaneous equations turn out to be fundamental in analyzing Mi's ideas about Time. I hasten to add that I am not rushing out to make my 'time machine', because I think it might fall to bits before it got past last week.

What about Tridel? If Mi wanted me to deduce this number there must have been a very important reason. Why deduce a number? The answer to this may lie in the *shape* of the number. Consider the first twin digit number of 11. This when divided by 3 gives Tridel. How might Mi recognize this? This can be done with a shape, but I'll use a line just for simplicity. Mark a line into eleven equal portions. Color the portions 1, 2, 3 and 4, and 8, 9, 10 and 11 in the same color, say red. The central portions are fewer so color them differently, say blue. It might be the balance of colors, or their interference that make a recognizable form. What is more important from our standpoint is that twin digit numbers most definitely form a pattern and it may be there that an answer could be found.

More about some that other time.

--------Epilogue-------

During my computations using the counts 81, 22 and 103 results have a very close resemblance to Tridel 1 along with Tridel 2 and this can also be achieved by using both Norman's and my first and last names.

You will remember that in an earlier chapter I mentioned the Crop Circles 'reply', where the SETI signal used the product number from the two prime numbers 73 and 23. Since 'threes' have been an important factor in this book, divide 1679 by three and the result is Norman's and my full name counts combined plus Tridel. No, I am not suggesting that any alleged 'reply' was meant for Norman and me, but it is a strange coincidence is it not?

I ask myself, *is* Tridel, or its geometrical shape equivalent, important in the Mi entity environment? Pi is used throughout our mathematics, therefore I wondered if in the Mi environment Tridel replaces Pi. If this were the case, I would expect to find further coincidences in support. After a large series of computations, the results clearly showed many further numerical coincidences. The details are not presented in this volume, but I will mention one or two.

One geometrical figure that I have been working on has an area, using Pi, of about 1696 units, but using Tridel the area is 1980 units. Subtracting 1696 and also the counts for 'Lawrencium' and 'Mira', the answer is 124. This just happens to be the count for the official name for Mira, Omicron Ceti. Now by going about it the other way and subtracting the 'location' counts for Lawrencium and Mira, 103 and 37, and also subtracting 1696, the answer coincides with the counts for Enki's three names, 144. This number seems to pop up everywhere.

There was one computation that was far more significant to me than the above two. The Earth moves around the Sun in what is almost a true circle in a period of approximately 365.25 days. The diameter of this circle is therefore about 116.263 days. By using Tridel on the numbers 1696 and 1980, the answer is about 116.265, the difference being a little under three minutes. Perhaps more important is that further theoretical work indicates that Tridel is associated the Sun / Earth movements involving twenty year intervals. So the conclusion is that Tridel may well be some kind of transformation device. In other computations I have clearly shown that both Tridel 1 and 2 have a close association with our already well-defined subject of Geometry.

I mention one of Norman's thoughts here. He suggests that our number system may be more advanced than Mi gives us credit for. If this is the case then we may well be solving problems which Mi cannot – and this is a good point on which to conclude this section.

It would appear that even during my sleeping hours my mind wasn't far from my 'Mi' problems. Sometimes I would find a solution to a particular problem in my dreams. During one time late at night, I had come up with the number 147 but couldn't think of what it might mean. I was tired and decided that it was time for bed; on this occasion, in a dream, I was walking down a long corridor with doors on both sides, very similar to those seen in large hotels. However, the walls and doors were undecorated and the same colour, a kind of 'off white'. There was a person, or persons, behind me and they were urging me to go to number 147. As I remember, I had quite a problem in finding the door marked 147, but I did eventually. As I opened the door I saw either a garden or a country scene, but what stood out most of all were two trees that were side by side and looked identical. At this point I woke up and went straight to my notes, thinking of the two trees being 'twin' trees. Norman's word 'twin' with a count of 66 coupled with the word count of 81 that appears in both Norman's and my name is 147. What a coincidence!

Moving on, on 2nd Feb.2003 Norman e-mailed me to say that he and his wife had heard the chimes again: clearly and the same as the originals, while watching TV the previous evening. So I took another look at the situation. It turns out that the numbers 66 and 81 occur again and it also happens that 66 has a connection to the Chimes expression. Norman's 'twin' and Chimes experience are clearly important. However, in addition, and using the notation in most books on Astronomy, we have two names for the same galaxy. In this case it is NGC1068 and M77 which, together, have a sequential count of 66:* a bit of a coincidence wouldn't you say? Just looking at the Chimes expression superficially, arrange the number sequence into a single number, 2244. Now, here is one of the simple reasons why I think that Norman's Chimes experience was due to Mi. Take Norman's full name count and multiply it by the count for 'Mi' and then divide the result by Tridel – the answer is...2244. Ah Ah – another coincidence.

Those of you with religious inclinations might like to consider some other possibilities. Look at some of the Biblical (or mythological if you prefer) names such as 'Jesus', 'Beelzebub', 'Devil', 'Lucifer', and 'Satan'. 'Devil', which contrary to common belief, is the only name mentioned originally associated with evil, a count of 52. This when added to Mi, 22, gives 74. Now the count for Lucifer is 74. However the original meaning for 'Lucifer' had nothing to do with evil. Both the planet Venus and the person Jesus (indirectly) can lay claim to the name 'Lucifer'. What is the count for 'Jesus'? 'Good lord'... it's 74. (Could one interpret this as Mi transforming the 'evil part' into the 'good part'?). 'Venus' has a count of 81, and adding 'Mi' to this would give 103. *Where have I seen that before*? Here is something even more interesting. 'Jesus' + 'Jehovah' (using conventional spelling), is equal to 'Enki' times Tridel, 143.

Satan was originally the spy spirit for God and the count for 'Satan' is 55. Add that to 22 to get 77. The other name has, at least, two variant spellings, Baalzebub and Beelzebub, who was the Lord of the Flies, for which I made no comparisons.

However, I found no further support, in the way of the numbers 74, 55 recurring for the suspicion of evil intentions: even if they had, surely the above interpretation would override any such suspicion. However, one does not necessarily have to believe in Biblical (or mythological) terms to believe in good and evil. Whilst there may be just-minded creatures in the universe, there may also be those who would cause havoc, given the chance. So we should be mindful that in doing certain things we may unleash some dark terrible force upon humanity. This is not necessarily my opinion but I feel it needs to be said. What *is more significant* to me, however, in highlighting these mythological aspects is this. In an earlier Chapter I proposed a theory about our language being engineered in some way. I think the above supports such a theory.

Okay, let us move on.

It is my opinion that unfortunately, our society has become one of opportunity. I see our buildings of ethics slowly crumbling under the strain of our ability to change our environment. For example, the temptation to clone a human being will, one day, be too great for someone to resist. This will set us on the path to who knows where.

If Time Travel becomes available then one day it will become a 'holiday attraction'.

*** "Announcing a Summer Sale to visit the age of the Dinosaurs. Stay in the Time Travel Dome Hotel where you can sit and watch the Tyrannosaurus Rex as it devours its prey while you eat your hamburger lunch in comfort and safety."***

Can you imagine that?!!!!

Yet, joking aside, I am sure you understand what I am saying. Theoretical Time Travel has not been the main aim of the analysis, but then, since it was me who had the 'Mi experience', one would hardly think otherwise. However, that Mi introduced the idea of Time Travel relative to four time zones does rank as at least intriguing. My assumption here is that when Mi 'communicated' to me the four categories of Time, Mi expected both Norman and I to pursue certain avenues based on our characteristics. That the 'data' so far accumulated is adequate for providing at least one possible solution, or more correctly, an interpretation of what Mi was trying to convey.

If I asked you the question, "What, actually, IS Time?" what would be your answer? Definitions are many, and to some extent, any answer depends on how one relates to the environment and our existence. To an Astronomer the answer may involve the overall structure of Our Universe; if you are a Physicist your answer may be more inclined towards micro-periods of atoms and subatomic particles. (Overall, Physicists consider that *Entropy* is increasing *Entropy* being the name given to the second law of Thermodynamics.) If you are Priest, a Nun or someone with a similar perspective, then your answer will, no doubt, involve a Divine Intervention. As for the rest of us, our answer may depend on how we have been conditioned and influenced by those I have mentioned as well as by others I haven't. I think the one thing that we would all agree upon is that we seem unable stop it; Time Marches On, Time Flies etc.

We talk about the 'arrow' of Time pointing in one direction, forward. Textbooks refer to Time is as a *scalar* quantity; a typical textbook definition goes something like '...time is that property which can be measured by clocks'. The problem is we then find ourselves having to define a clock, atomic clocks, clocks depending on a certain wavelength and so on. I hardly think that you can put any of these in your living room.

If you are a 'Logical Positivist', then there is no way back and the only direction is forward, and since the future has not yet been determined there is no future to go to. If you an 'Empiricist' then experimental, empirical quantities are the qualities you will follow. (The Special Theory of Relativity is a good example, where one can talk about travelling at velocities close that of light, and finding on your return that you have aged at a slower rate than those left behind. The 'positivist' might then argue that your own 'internal clock' has still functioned normally and that you have aged according to that situation. The 'empiricist' will argue that it is possible to slow time down. This is indeed a very long debate, and I don't intend to enter into it here.)

Temperature is defined as a scalar quantity but however, associated with this *scalar field* there is a *vector* quantity, so a discussion on Time might follow the same lines. Time as defined in theories concerning Entropy (looked it up yet?), on the whole preclude any suggestion of Time Travel.

As an analogy, suppose you have a motor car that has three forward gears only. Then quite clearly to drive it and expect to be able to reverse while performing a three point turn is out of the question. To reverse the car you would need to get out of the car and *push* it backwards, or ask someone else to help. Analogously, this is what is required about our definition of Time. We might smash atoms to 'see inside' but perhaps for Time we need to 'go outside' of our definition to find the answers we seek.

At this moment you are reading this sentence, but in the same moment various other activities are being performed by, perhaps, other members of your family. Extending this further, events all over the world are proceeding within that same moment. If we could freeze this moment, as in a photograph, quite clearly what we have is a 'slice' of Time. This means that Time, in our present definition is a 'one-many relation'. ('Relation', rather than 'relationship', is a mathematical term in this regard. For example, being a parent of more than one child is a 'one-many relation'). We apply statistical procedures to 'one-many' problems, and talk of the probability of an event occurring, and statistical results are interpreted using the area of some particular *distribution* or graph. Today's society relies very much on statistical values, but it is not the route I shall be taking here.

Enter Mi. Mi stated that everything had a C.T. Signature, which seems to have the implication that everything is uniquely identified, giving everything some unique Time-object value. If this is the case, then this at once takes us outside our current definition, because everything has a history. Let's take a closer look at what this would mean.

We speak of a 'world line' which is the path taken by an object through space-time. If two objects experienced exactly the same events at exactly the same point in the world lines, we might well end up with a type of Siamese twin syndrome. However, fortunately this doesn't happen too often, and so this world line idea isn't really so far from Mi's C.T.

However, Mi suggested that we rely too much on some things and do not interact with our environment enough to develop our senses. Now, I do not intend to debate here whether or not we, or any other life form (including Mi), are capable of such a thing, or whether it is even desirable to do so; this is a completely different question. The point is, however, that if we all possess a unique C.T. value then our 'slice' of Time becomes a complete set of individual, three-dimensional time 'chambers'. Within each 'chamber', Time explicitly defines the contents, and although some modification may be allowed, there will be a fundamental 'time gene' (or to use my own mathematical term, a Repeatable Relative Function, RRF for short). This will determine the development of the contents of the C.T. By Mi's definition of the four Time categories, C.T. must be an 'active' type. If C.T. has the property of being in the present, and when a moment has passed, C.T. becomes placed in the past ('wherever' that might be), then we have the problem of how the C.T. obtains access to the future category. Another question that needs an answer is that if the present has a signature via C.T., this implies that the past also has a signature. Does the future and 'unused' Time have a Non C.T. signature?

The idea of a 'signature' is a common term in scientific subjects and you will find for example, one signature describing our own space-time continuum is (+, -, -, -) while that of the Wave equation in 3-D is (+, +, +, -). The two signatures are clearly opposite to one another, and I wonder if we are back in the realm of mirror imaging. Is it possible that Mi was aware of this? I had been searching for a type of signature in the material, but had failed to find one and Norman was unaware of this. So you can imagine my surprise when Norman had his experience, and from the information he gave, I was able to deduce, as you have already seen, the Chimes expression which has the signature (+, -, -, +).

One problem has been however, that the Chimes expression is balanced, or symmetrical, and I have been unable to make certain negative derivations. This might be an example of where the Chimes expression and Mi's ideas take us away from our usual system of analysis. I could scrap one idea and simply employ another to derive the desired features. For example, I could just rearrange the signs so that I would use a signature of (-,+,-,+), but I haven't found anything to suggest that I should use this procedure. Perhaps a mirror image of the original but this still does not give the negative derivations. The Chimes expression and Mi's ideas are all I have, and I must preserve their integrity. Even when I use the tetrads I end up with a circle divided into four quadrants with the lower left quadrant empty. So it seems that one of the Time zones *may* not be available to us. Using the Chimes expression I finally ended up with a system of rotating magnetic fields which required a large amount of energy, and I am not sure whether such magnetic field strengths are achievable by scientists yet. Such high energies also pose other big problems for engineers, and again, I am not sure if the technology is available yet. Having said all that, I have found another interpretation that involves other ideas but will not give any details here, except to say that Tridel and the count for 'time', 47, are very much involved.

Another point I have also omitted is any mention of how one might select a certain period and be transported to it. I think it unlikely that one would see instants 'passing by' and then simply 'get off' at the desired instant. It is more likely that a selection would be made prior to any intended journey, and it is Tridel that might provide a possible answer to this problem. It is in this context that the number 111 (from the English and Thai languages mentioned earlier) may have its place of importance. (This number is also mentioned below but concerning another, quite unexpected set of coincidences). Nor have I ignored the force that nothing in *our* universe can escape, Gravity. It has such a profound effect on us that there is probably no study of it that also doesn't at some point, include Time. Anything that has mass has an associated gravitational field (which is one of the reasons it becomes so difficult to unify macro and subatomic levels since some particles are said to be 'massless'). To the ordinary reader who, I am sure has heard of 'Black Holes', 'Electrons' and perhaps even 'Quarks', such things should be just opposite ends of the same rod. Perhaps Mi's C.T. can help here.

Your body as a whole will have a certain value of C.T. Your skeleton will have a C.T. value and so too will your muscular make up. No problem, add the C.T.'s together to arrive at an overall C.T. Things get a little more complicated when we start thinking about individual bones and organs, and by the time we arrive at a blood corpuscle, the C.T. probably bears no resemblance to the original C.T. We haven't even started to consider genetic structures. Yet all belong to your one body and therefore must have a definite coordinated relationship. Perhaps if I can solve the problem of Mi's C.T. maybe I can claim the modern sought after prize called 'The Theory of Everything'....I wish Mi had left his e-mail address. Joking aside, in terms of Mi's ideas, Time, Gravity and Magnetism (electromagnetism) are all connected. There is at least one possible interpretation of the 'flow' of time that will be different from our own current philosophy. The 'flow' or arrow of Time may point in one direction, but that direction may be *towards* us. That is to say that our dimension possesses the ability to attract time and time will thus flow *through* us. In recent years there has been a lot publicity concerning (Super)String Theory, otherwise known as The Theory of Everything, T.O.E., and it may well be that the ellipsoids I have mentioned, coupled with the idea of C.T., could have some connection with String Theory.

I have mentioned previously the Special Theory of Relativity (S.R.), and though I have no intentions of discussing this theory, I do want to highlight certain parts that might be useful here.

It is now well known that subatomic particles that have a certain 'life span' when at 'rest', if accelerated to a considerable fraction of light speed exist for a longer period, according to the equipment at 'rest'. The idea is that the particle's own 'clock' will continue similarly as it did at rest, but being highly accelerated the particle travels through many more 'rest' periods, subsequently equipment at 'rest' registers an increase in the span of existence. This is the principle of Time Dilation. In everyday language, suppose you are in your space ship and moving at, say 0.999 of the speed of light. In your space ship your chronometer registers a round trip of one year at this speed, yet on your return your friends will say that you have been away for over twenty-two years. So here is a situation where you could travel into the future, that is, someone else's future, not yours. In addition, having made the return journey, simply reversing direction does not take you into the past.

Also, this form of 'time travel' has a few other undesirable features. During the round trip mentioned, all that you have done is sit in your spacecraft, maybe for some research project take a few measurements, but basically you have probably made very little personal progress. Your family, friends and everyone else have aged twenty-two years, but during that time what have they done? Perhaps the price you have paid for gaining those extra years above everyone else may be too high. On the positive side, someone who is terminally ill may benefit by taking such a trip and perhaps finding that on return advances in treatment have been made or even a cure has been found.

On the whole, however, this is not really what we have in mind when we talk about Time Travel. We think of travelling to a desired point, Past or Future, and then returning to the starting point. The standard form of the S.R. equation concerning Time tells us that when we reach the speed of light we have to divide the square root of zero, by zero which of course, on any calculator or computer will result in an 'error' sign. Negating the time difference in the equation works equally well and travelling backward through time might be similarly affected. We didn't, however, use the equations to reverse the Time parameter, and the suggestion is that the speed of light is only part of the equation, or may not be involved at all.

Mi said that everything has a C.T. signature, so I therefore must assume that every given moment that will become the past has a signature also. Now, as I am restricting the discussion to the Earth only, what could we say about the Earth's C.T. signature? During Norman's own study he came across a certain feature which apparently peaks every twenty years, on the third year. The particular years Norman refers to are 1943 and 1983, and the feature referred to is called the Earth's Biorhythm (see book reference). Extending this to other years we would have 1903, 1923, 1943, 1963, 1983, and 2003. I made some comparisons, using a twenty year gap, that is, 20, 40, 60, 80 and 100 years, so that there are five points, 1903 to 1923 (the zero point), 1923 to 1943 and so on. I did not choose figures for the intervals because one feature of my statistical CurveExpert program [actual spelling] is that it can calculate an appropriate interval. My program's estimated increments for the intervals were all multiples of Tridel. Now, *that is* an amazing coincidence! The result is a straight line.

The main point, however, is that with increasing years, the graph is decreasing, and indeed the year 2163 gives a value of about 1% lower than last century, and if these figures do relate to the Earth's Biorhythm, what value represents an environment *unsuitable* for human habitation? With regard to Time Travel, it may be possible that these figures relate to the C.T. signature and could be used for selecting which period one wants to travel to. Before any selection can be effected, however, we first have to find a way to stay within a given moment and not to progress to the next, thus vanishing from view in the next moment. This is the next, and final, topic concerning Mi's ideas.

To determine a Time Field we need to determine a vector field connected to it. The Theory of Relativity imposes a hidden restriction upon this idea, but previous examples imply that the closer one gets to the velocity of light, the more 'time periods' one uses. Now, since everything is in a state of movement (movement at the atomic level, we move, the Earth moves, the Solar System moves and so on) it becomes possible that it is the movement of everything that is using up 'time periods'. This then raises the question as to whether Time is actually moving at all, and it is the existence of everything that cause 'ripples' in Time.

Finding a 'stationary point' in the Time field is necessary. We do not need to get into a big debate similar to one about whether the impact of your toe with a table leg was the result of the table leg moving towards your toe or your toe moving towards the table leg. The pain is undeniable. In other words, the consideration of whether the vector field and stationary points are due to our existence, or that of Time, can be left to another discussion.

The important point is to give a Time Field designation, and based on theoretical work the possibilities are 22, Tridel and multiples of Tridel. Indeed, at a very early stage I found that Tridel seems to be related, mathematically, to the Earth and Moon and therefore may also have some connection to the remarks I made at the bottom of page 153. During certain computations the number 16 turns up in a variety of ways, not least in connection with the Chimes expression. Indeed, the fourth position of the original expression is '$4d$' equals 16 when $d = 4$ as in the fourth letter of the alphabet. The number 16 may refer to the 16 numbers that make up the tetrads, or simply two times eight. The Chimes expression has another important property where the total is 1536.

Now, one set of the combined simultaneous and Chimes equations renders three items redundant (due to a mathematical theorem) and the 'd' position of the Chimes expression becomes the 'controlling external' item of the resulting value. For example, placing a '0' in this position gives the whole a value of '0'. Thus, the three simultaneous equations given to Mi, plus the Chimes expression provide one theoretical route to controlling whatever vectors we decide to include; more coincidences turn up using this procedure. For example, a figure when used in the Time Dilation equation of S.R. that results in Pi years, gives the result of 111 a figure mentioned earlier (page 78) and will be seen again shortly.

However, the foregoing are only intermediates of my GATE equations proper, and the next stage relies on the relationship between these and figures obtained by rotating the twenty four tetrads.

If I have given the impression that I have solved all of the problems concerned with the present material, I do apologize. I haven't. For example, several results suggest that an angle of 45° is involved thus giving an interpretation similar to that of the water ripple. Other indications suggest a larger angle supporting an idea of perhaps 'warping' out of the light cone of S.R., but I have restricted the analysis to our own locality, where using a 'time line' relevant to the Earth might be reasonable. What if one is far out in space, how can Earth's 'time line' be accessed from there? This is a good place to conclude this discussion on Time.

'…can everywhere to twenty four…'. This phrase, when I think about it, still makes me smile. I wonder what we would say if we encountered a stranger in the local restaurant, bar, or other social gathering, and we asked 'where do live?' If one got the reply '…can everywhere to twenty four…'. I am sure that some of us would wish we hadn't asked the question in the first place. This somewhat cryptic response from Mi rather indicates that Mi thought I was incapable of understanding the true answer, or Mi was incapable of giving it in terms that I could understand. On the other hand, Mi may have wanted to keep the location secret, not wanting to be pursued by crowds of us humans. If that was the case why not just refuse to answer?

However, there is another possible interpretation given Mi's apparent lack of expertise with the English language, which may involve Time. We could, ourselves, exist everywhere if we had the appropriate life support equipment, though at present our level of technology would preclude certain environments. Mi life technology may be advanced enough to allow travel to any environment. When Mi added the 'twenty four' perhaps Mi meant up until Mi was twenty-four 'something' of age. There are reasons for me suggesting this avenue of thought. Multiply both Norman's and my birth years together, then multiply the result by 22, representing Mi. Now multiply by 24 and then by twice Tridel. The answer is 14.48241×10^9. This figure, fourteen thousand four hundred and eighty two million years is within the current (highest) estimate of the age of our known universe. I am not suggesting that this is Mi's age, though I am not suggesting it isn't, either.

It is true to say that other birth years, those of our parents for example, would achieve similar results, and that the above results are by no means unique. What is interesting is that the year 1968, mentioned previously in connection with Norman and I, gives a result that is the closest to the age of the highest estimate, while 1969 does go beyond it. Year 1761 is the year that gives a result just inside the lowest estimate of 12×10^9 years. Thus there is a range of 207 years, a figure that would seem not very useful here – but wait. Not Enki again? Enki + Ea + Nudimmud = 144 + sequential additions = 207

Be that as it may, and I am sure you will agree that this is just about as much Time as we can handle, we do have to stop and ask ourselves, what does it mean? Well, the first obvious point is that Tridel is a common factor, which really confirms my theory that Tridel is in some way involved with Time. Indeed, since I have linked Tridel with Mi's ideas about Time, then surely the above results imply that Tridel is that all-important bridge between our concept of Time and Mi's.

Changing the topic of conversation, I want to clear up what may have appeared a bit of a mystery to some. Where did my simultaneous equations come from?

Did Mi find these useful (in Mi's own way) in providing answers to questions I would be thinking about? It is possible that the first equation set could have been anticipated by Mi because involves answers of simply 1 and 2, but I doubt whether this would be true of the second equation set. Mi would have had to 'encourage' or 'insert' the set prior to my presenting them to the 'image'. As I mentioned before, during the experience I did feel as though certain ideas were being 'inserted', so it is not beyond the realms of possibility that these equations were 'encouraged' at that time. Actually, it turns out that Mi wouldn't have to 'give' the equations to me at all, because I **already knew them prior** to the first 'crying' in 1976.

Before the meditation session where I contacted the 'image' of the Mi entity, I must have written down, and memorized, what I intended to ask. I cannot actually confirm this because such notes would have been with those that were 'lost'. Another possibility might be that Mi prompted them from the depths of my memory. It was not until I started to work on the figures from Norman's Chimes experience that I realized it was about the late 1960's or early 70's that I had been studying simultaneous equations. The one with three unknowns that was presented to the Mi 'image' was one of the examples I had studied.

However, if this is true then there should be a most definite relationship with the Chimes expression. In fact these two do have a mathematical connection and it is here that I find another way to derive Tridel. Herein lays the main reason why I think that Norman's Chimes experience was due to Mi. I omit the mathematical details and just state the result. By replacing the letters *a, b, c, d* in the Chimes expression with the solutions to the equations given to Mi, the answer is 22, the count for 'Mi'. Not only that, but when all the individual numbers that make up the solutions to the equations given to Mi are added sequentially, the answer is also 22. Norman himself was very skeptical about my theory that his Chimes experience was due to Mi, but after looking at my computations in full he agreed that they presented a convincing argument. One wonders that had Norman remained in Thailand would he have seen the entity too.

There was one further point that interested me concerning the Chimes expression. The format of the expression means that an answer of 2 is not unique. Indeed, there are a great many, if not infinite amount, of possible solutions. So my question was – is there another set of values that would give a result of 2, but with the additional condition that figures so obtained have some resemblance to figures herein? The answer is yes, but I omit the detail because the mathematics goes beyond ordinary arithmetic. The problem is basically a question of dimensions between the Chimes expression and the simultaneous equations. What seems to happen is that the equations I gave to Mi limit the scope of the Chimes expression with the result that '*a*', '*b*' and '*c*' of the expression involve division by the number 41, with yet another identity of Tridel being found.

Mi's word 'apovolintive', count of 160, is reminiscent of the word 'voluntary' which has a word count of 148 and this is 144+4; alone it doesn't mean much. The first interesting point is that by finding the first sequential count of 'voluntary' and then the second (40 & 4), dividing 160 by the first gives the second and vice versa. The second point is that by subtracting the second sequential count from 148 we end up with our 'old friend' 144. However, what may well be the reason for Mi communicating this word is that by using 160, the count for 'Mi' and my name count the result is a small fraction above Norman's name count!

This really brings me to the end my meeting with the Mi entity, though there are still a couple of interesting 'twists' to come. I will refer to just two more coincidences. Multiplying Norman's full name count with mine gives a result 68068, which, just by coincidence, is such a well-balanced figure with 'Cetus' at each end. Now add the mirror image, 86086, and the answer is 154154. Now divide this by my name count, and the answer is 847, which is Norman's name count plus the mirror image. Lastly, but by no means least, divide 154154 by the number I dreamt about, 147, then divide this answer by Tridel squared (Tridel times Tridel) and the answer is the count for Mira Ceti. Using Tridel 2, Lawrencium (plus its Atomic number) can also be computed which brings us right back to the beginning.

Norman has a great deal more experience in investigating Strange Encounters than I have, but here the entity Mi has involved him in something else, of which I mention a little in my final paragraphs. Once again, Norman has his own ideas on that. Whether we will ever know, or come realize the true meaning of my experience, is something that I think about every day. Mi is now part of my life. Oh, I may not be able to remember or touch those earlier feelings that I must have had, but the experience has changed my life. I don't just think Mi is there. I don't just believe Mi is there. I **know** Mi is there

The three equations that I gave to the entity Mi may not have been arbitrary on my part, and perhaps Mi orchestrated events from there. I had totally forgotten I had used them in studies a quarter of a century before (I hardly think I should be criticized for that) and this may have been Mi's way of reminding me. I find it interesting that these equations can be solved by another route (not given herein), and the number of steps taken to do so is *eight*. The drawings I made that resembled the design on a shirt I have, led to the musical connotations and the star Mira, the factor Tridel being not only represented in our chemical make up, but also in the same constellation in which Mira resides. Is it possible that the musical ideas concerned with my shirt design was an indication that there was about to be musical interlude, Norman's Chimes experience? From that, The Chimes expression was derived which provided me with the missing link in theoretical work, a situation that Norman was quite unaware of at the time.

Then, more than two years after our experiences Norman came up with yet something else that I was totally unprepared for.

Norman had been studying the situation concerning the laboratory at Montauk (Long Island USA) and the Philadelphia Experiment and during August of 2002 Norman, in an e-mail to me, asked for my ideas concerning the dates 12-8-1943 and 12-8-1983. My reply (in words) went something like this: - *

"The sequential count for the first date equals 28 and that of the send is 32. The number of days to the 12th of August is 224. 224 divided by 28 and 32 equals 8 and 7 respectively. The final sequential count for eight plus seven is 6. Divide the interval of 40 years by 6 and the answer is 6.6666666...or Tridel plus 3.

Next find the total number of days in 40 years and divide by your [Norman's] name count and the result is a fraction above the count for Enki [remember that Norman introduced Enki into the analysis].

Lastly, the number of days in 40 years minus the product of your [Norman's] name count and that of Enki and the result is 24 [Mi's '...to twenty four...' perhaps?] This would seem to indicate that you are associated with Enki."

What I did not realize was that Norman's original question about dates was in connection to his study concerning Montauk and the Philadelphia Experiment. Once again Norman and I were in constant contact and the numerical coincidences began to appear one after the other.

Firstly, the name count of 'Edward Cameron' plus 'Duncan Cameron' has a total of 250; subtract this from Norman's full name count and the answer is 124 we have seen before as the word count for Omicron Ceti (or it might be Edward Cameron). This initial coincidence suggests that we should take s closer look.

Alfred Bielek allegedly had some connection to Edward Cameron so by forming the sum (E.C. + Mi) multiplied by (A.B. + Mi) divided by Norman's name count and my own the answer almost equal to <u>eight</u> times Tridel.

Next, subtract 'Edward Cameron' from Norman's first and last names and the answer is the same as the result on the bottom of the previous page, 32. Now use Norman's two middle names with the combined count of E.C. and D.C. and the answer is again 32. If that isn't some kind of merry-go-round I don't know what is but it doesn't end there. Add these two results together and the answer is 64, which is 8 times 8, establishing another connection to the number 8. Perhaps more appropriately, 64 is also the word count for 'Eldridge'.

If Alfred Bielek came into existence at the age of 1 in 1927, then the theoretical birth year would be the same as Norman's, 1926. Adding the counts for Norman's name, Edward Cameron and Duncan Cameron the answer equals eight times the count for Mira Ceti or sixteen times the count for Enki. However by subtracting my name and the count for Cetus (remember that Mira Ceti is in the Constellation of Cetus) from the above sum the answer is equal Norman's name count. Another merry-go-round?

--------Epilogue-------

Fort Hero, where the site of the Montauk laboratory was, came from (General) Andrew Hero, word count 111. The number 111 first appeared as the combination of the English and Thai alphabets (see page 78) then in the 'reaction chamber' (see page 83).

There are a large number of further coincidences but I omit them here; suffice to say that there now seemed to be a connection between Montauk Laboratory, the Philadelphia Experiment and my Mi experience, with Norman as the essential link.

That there seems to be a connection with water (Cetus) in my experience, was it possible that there was for Montauk also? Norman was quick to point out that Long Island is a peninsular so the connection seemed obvious, and of course the ship 'Eldridge' also had a definite connection. However, there are a great number of ships and peninsulas throughout the world, probably some with name counts that would also fit. What I was looking for was some kind of rarity involving Long Island. Once again I employed word counts and 'Long Island' equals 107; Long Island facing an ocean so 'Long Island' minus 'ocean' equals the count for 'Thailand'. Apart from the fact that I live in Thailand to make any kind of 'prediction' involving the two places might prove difficult, so the next thing I did was to look at the mirror image of the word counts. 'Water' 67, 76 and 'ice' 17, 71; 'steam' 58, 85 and 'ocean' 38, 83. By using the mirror image numbers in the sums a result of 55 seem to reoccur.* Dividing by Tridel gives a result of 15, for which I found no use (although by a similar process it would equal 'twin'). What about the number 55 as it is? By *coincidence* the word 'glacier' also equals fifty five, so I thought that there might be a connection here. Many places have seen glacial activity throughout history, but if it was to be meaningful here it would have to be special in some way.

Another thought that occurred to me was that, if there is connection to Norman how do I could find it? Where do I look? I had deduced 'glacier' basically from water and Long Island; very well then let's just add the numbers and their mirror images and – well, well, well, what a surprise, we end up with Norman's full name count.*

170

--------Epilogue-------

However, Norman's interests, at this particular time, lay with the Montauk / Philadelphia affair so how does this fit in with glacial activity? Norman introduced Enki and the other name, Ea has meanings in English relating to water (first appeared in 1781 and it was in the same year that water was first synthesized). The planet Uranus (word count of 94) was discovered in 1781, and is thought to have large quantities of water below its surface. By subtracting the count for Enki from 'Uranus' we get 55 again. Since Enki has made yet another appearance, I thought to use the word count for 'Mi' and wondered if Tridel might be here somewhere also and had some success.

Based on these figures I suggested to Norman that there might have been glacial activity at Montauk at around ten thousand years ago, which is very recent in terms of history. Consequently Norman sent me material regarding Long Island (from the Website www.newsday.com) and it seems experts believe that Long Island had glacial activity around twenty two thousand to eleven thousand years ago, which again historically speaking is very recent. Even in the number of years, twenty-two and eleven are represented here. So it turns out that my approximation was not that far out, but more importantly it convinced me that indeed my Mi experience and the Montauk affair are connected and I think the vital link is indeed Norman.

From the information that I received from Norman via The Montauk Pulse', it seems that the Montauk 'time line' coincides with the death of a daughter of an Indian chief. Her name was Heather Flower, and if you complete a word count on this name you will find it is our 'old friend, 144,

I will mention just one more point, which concerns the year 1963. The years 1943 and 1983 turn out to be important with regard to the Eldridge and Montauk connection and obviously 1963 is the mid-point year. I made some calculations involving another Tridel related formula, for the 'biorhythmic' 1803 to 2003. The only forty year period which gives the mid-point year as the result is that of 1943 to 1983 (the figure is actually 1962.966). Indeed, performing the procedure on 1963 alone results in the same figure, while this relationship does not appear with the other 'biorhythmic' years. Then something else turned up. When I did certain graphical computations involving 390 years the year 1943 just happens to produce a figure very close to Tridel 2. This suggested to me that Mi was trying to guide me to a certain result and I believe that the result has been found, but there is more work to be done. As if this was not enough, when I turned the figures upside down, so to speak, I found that by inserting my own curve fit formula ('user defined model') which was based on Tridel, my computer selected it as the best fit formula. It did so only by a miniscule amount but it outranked all of the program's statistical formulae. I have also used the Chimes expression for another set of figures, and that was ranked second.

Perhaps a very important question might be something like – what makes August 12th, day 224, special? I could say, 'Mira' plus 'Enki' plus 144, or perhaps 'Lawrence' ('Oliver') with Tridel and Enki. Interesting possibly, but I hardly think that Mira, Enki, Norman and I contribute significantly to the Earth's biorhythm. However these numbers may be pointers and suggest a route to the answer.

What could someone say about the Earth's rotation around the Sun even if they were observing from outer space? Then, one might ask the question 'what can be deduced about day number 224?' Using dates are taken from the same source where I found the 'Mee' area on the Moon, which uses Sidereal Time, in a non leap year day 224 just happens to be 'Mira' (41) days before the Autumn Equinox, September 22nd and 'Enki' times Tridel days (143) after the Spring Equinox, March 22nd. (Equinox dates vary between the 20st and 23rd; I have simply used the figure that coincides with the count for 'Mi') What is the day number of March 22nd? It is 'Lawrence' or 'Oliver' (81).

Using Mira Ceti and Lawrencium name and sequential counts, (no sequential count for Lawrencium's 103) the answer is 285 and taking this as a day number, dividing by day 224 the answer is almost exactly to the figure for Tridel 2. However, I would say that every day is unique in some way, so is Mi trying to tell us something specific here? I will not go into the mathematical detail, but further coincidences occur when using the above figures in the equations of an electromagnetic field. More coincidences are exposed but will appear in the next book.

Late in 2004 there came yet another 'twist'. In the early chapters I mentioned that Norman went to America during 2000, and when he was there stayed with a friend in the town of Mena. During 2004 when Norman was researching various aspects, he was told by another unrelated source that the Indian Tribe at Montauk had their origins in the Mintaka Indians of Mena. Now, I knew nothing about this Indian tribe but did recognize the name 'Mintaka' in the same way that I had recognized the Latin term 'mira'. Mintaka is the name given to the star Delta Orionis. Unlike Mira, Mintaka is derived from Arabic and two other designations are M.78 and NGC 2068; we have already seen that M.77 is NGC 1068 showing 'similarities' in the designations.

The word count for 'Mintaka' is the same as that for 'Thailand', 69 and 'Mena' is 33, which by coincidence is the same as 'Delta Orionis' divided by Tridel. The product produces a number with familiar digits, 2277, a nice looking twin set. What is more important to me is that when 'Mena' is translated according to the matrix code I used for four letter words (see page 66/67), and then used this as a number it directly connects to Norman's full name count.*

Now, I ask – where am I in all this? One more time, use the matrix code number for Mena but now divide by Tridel then take Norman's name count plus 'Lawrencium' plus 'Mi', subtract the figure obtained from Mena and Tridel and the answer is my name count!

These surely must rank as an amazing 'coincidences' but if you are still doubtful about these computations let me go one step further. Multiply the individual digits of the number 847 (see page 167) together, 8 times 4 times 7; the answer is 224, precisely the day number of August 12th (non leap year). Now things really do get interesting because adding my full name count to the count for Lawrencium and Atomic number plus the mirror image of the result equals 808. Doing the same for 'Long Island' equals 808, but even more interesting, when 808 is added to Tridel times Tridel and then *dividing* this result is by Tridel the answer is 224.03. How close is that? Wouldn't it just complete the picture if the Chimes expression could be also accounted for? The Chimes expression in its original form would be equal to 2, and dividing 808 by this brings us back to the original counts. Simple isn't it!

There is considerably more that I could add to these coincidences but it would take us into matters that I have not mentioned in this volume. Suffice to say that all of the main 'characters' can be derived from the above and much more, but then, once more, I was to get yet another surprise from Norman.

During early 2005 Norman gave me further details of a second book about Montauk, 'Montauk Revisited; Adventures in Synchronicity' by Preston B. Nichols and Peter Moon. Names given here were not previously known to me since up to this date I hadn't read either of the books (I know, I should have done eh?), but even so certain things started to happen. Since the authors were somehow connected to this study I thought that familiar figures might be derived from their name counts. I was not able to obtain the middle name of Preston Nichols so unfortunately I couldn't include his name in the analysis and though the name 'Peter Moon' did give some indications of being vaguely coincidental I really wasn't satisfied. For example, I used Tridel to the power of 7 and in another case, Tridel to the power of 3 multiplied by 3 squared; although they are all about the number three it still seemed like a misuse of the 'three principle', plus there wasn't anything direct or that stood out. So I asked Norman if this author had another name. He did have (but I have not asked for permission to give it here), and straight away…Norman's full name count minus the author's name equals Lawrencium plus its Atomic number.

There is a little more to the story involving other people connected with the Montauk laboratory, but the situation remained confused because of what I can only say was a mysterious 'merry-go-round' concerning names. Nonetheless, in the overall picture figures related to my theoretical studies began to appear. I gave a sigh and said something to the equivalent of "that's it, I have to read these books", and in October of 2005 I received them in the post. Almost at once I found more coincidences and I list just a few here that I read.

Montauk.

An extract from a document collected from the abandoned Montauk Laboratory has two entries of the 23rd January. You may remember that this is the birthday of both my mother and my Thai wife.

The age range of certain children is from 6 to 22 years, exactly the numbers that I used to produce Tridel.

Philadelphia Experiment

The USS Eldridge's number was DE 173, D+E+173 equals 182, which is my full name count. There are also coincidences using the counts for 'USS Eldridge' plus D+E+173.

Using this with a man whom may have had two names, one being the Mexican equivalent of the American name, or from two men, one Mexican and one American with the same names in their native tongues, Tridel can be exactly derived.

Even the names of the places connected to the USS Eldridge produce coincidences. The list goes on and on. Having mentioned Long Island previously, reminds me that Long Island is the home of the research facility, Brookhaven National Laboratory (BNL). The research at BNL covers a broad spectrum of subjects, including Biology, Medicine and Particle Physics. The Particle Physics team at BNL did research involving Quarks and shared a Nobel Prize for this during the 1970's. There seems to be a 'three family' for the subatomic particles arrangement and one wonders whether the 'three's' herein are relevant. Indeed, there appears to be a connection between the answers of the *three* simultaneous equations given to Mi, Lawrencium, along with the word count for 'Mi' and the reaction involving the production of Lawrencium. Could this mean that Mi lives in subatomic environment?

As a final note on this section it is worth mentioning a thought that Norman had. Could Mi's 'everywhere to twenty-four' mean 'everywhere two twenty-four'? It certainly sounds similar, and the 12th of August 1943 was day 224 but unfortunately there is now, no way of checking. I can only assume that during my 'communication' with the entity I had a reason for writing '...to...' and not '...two...'.

--------Epilogue-------

I now regret to say that there are even more questions to answer there were before! Was Mi connected to the Montauk / Philadelphia experiments and if so in what way? Is Mi connected to one of those unfortunate sailors who were aboard the Eldridge and perhaps sent through some dimensional barrier? If so why use the name 'Mi'? What is Mi trying to tell us about the Montauk / Philadelphia experiment? Why try at all, and why bring Norman and yours truly into it? What is this apparent connection between Norman's American friend, Norman and me? Why..? It would seem I have opened a floodgate of questions that I think I have little chance in answering, let alone trying to understand what happened to me. Even the Roswell incident of July 1947 has produced coincidences which require further study. (Oh, by the way, Norman, the word 'apovolintive' (page 167) might well connect your name count to the Philadelphia Experiment. Just thought I'd let you know.)

Be that as it may, I will make a few concluding remarks. It seems to me that Mi is restricted, at the very least, in entering our type of universe and at most may not be able to enter or exist in our universe at all.

I no longer think of Time as I did before, nor do I see it in same respect as did Einstein and other contemporaries. To me, Time is no longer a set of passing or future periods, with the present somehow locked between the others. To me Time is the essence from which all the other physical qualities are born. I suppose one might see the analogy with the oceans of our beautiful planet. The oceans of water are our one resource without which our form of life here would not exist. We draw our total existence from this one item.

Some may think that Mi has something to do with the 'other Larry' mentioned in the first chapter, though surely any such creature would have better command of English than what Mi illustrated. Suppose the 'other Larry' had replied to my question of whereabouts, ' …ruof ytnewt ot erehwyreve nac…' , that really would have stumped me.

I have had some benefit from the experience. For example, how often does one think about the past and would like to change this or that. I no longer have that irritation on my mind. I now feel that whatever I have done in my life, right or wrong, has set me on the path to where I am today. In my meditations I no longer seek contentment, because I have found it. I can, at long last, appreciate and understand what my father and his friend were trying to teach me when they set me on my path. I can move on in my thoughts without having first to sweep away the dust of yesteryear that frequently accumulates in our lives. If the opportunity to revisit the past presented itself to me, where previously it might have been tempting I would now, most definitely, decline the offer. Like many before me, (and I am sorry to say, probably many after me), my account of the experience will be viewed with much skepticism by many people. This is something I will have to live with.

This then, trying to unfold the meaning, is my legacy to the experience with the entity known as Mi. The question as to why Mi bothered to contact us at all still remains a mystery. If Mi had wanted us to fathom Time and Mi's whereabouts why not just give us a map and a few direct basic ideas? Perhaps Mi expected us to be more intelligent and resourceful and build our own space/time machine; thus we would become famous. In that case why not give us the 'blueprints', and save us a lot of trouble?

At the beginning of this Epilogue I mentioned the first criticism of this book and it is now time to discuss the second criticism, the derivation of coincidences from the names. Perhaps many people will argue that is all they are, coincidence. Some may suggest that it is impossible for a letter count and a word count to have any influence on external, physical events. If this is the impression I have given then I apologize. I believe that Mi wanted me to uncover these coincidences *because they run parallel* to certain actual situations; situations that may be governed by a totally different set of circumstances. Take Tridel for example. Now, I have no more idea of what circumstances and formulations are used by secret government projects than any other ordinary person, but it is possible that a figure equivalent to Tridel may be present in some theory or construction somewhere; likewise some of the other numbers important herein. My GATE equations may be simplified parallel versions of some used elsewhere. The important question is why would Mi want me to do this? Some skeptic may say that what I have written and suggested is absurd, and that languages have evolved *naturally*. I would remind this person of one 'peculiarity' of what is currently theorized in the realm of Quantum Mechanics. The results of a certain repeatable experiment prompted the theory that the electron may be in two places at once, and a famous scientist wrote of this by saying "...I hope you can accept nature as She is – absurd." To my skeptic I have to say that no matter how many times my computations are repeated the result is always the same.

You will have perhaps noticed that I, personally, use the term 'coincidence' where perhaps others may have used the term 'synchronicity'. Synchronistic matters really deal with *events* in time but I could not claim that all of my derivations fall under that heading. I am not suggesting that, for the material in this book, someone using the term 'synchronicity' would be wrong to do so, just that perhaps I am being a little cautious in my terminology.

It would seem to me now that Norman's input has been so important that I feel the experience was directed towards **him** and not me. This might seem like an odd statement to make since it was me who had the visit from the Mi entity, but I could not have made the important deductions, and connections to Tridel, without Norman's introductions of 'twin', (the amazing) Enki and the all important Chimes experience formula. In any case, Norman was in Thailand before me, and one wonders whether he too might have had the Mi experience had he stayed. This is not the end of the story because at the time of writing Norman is engaged in another case study of a different kind, yet the coincidences persist. Norman gave to me the names of three places important in his study, and they all have exactly the same word count which just happens to be the same count as 'Mira'. The coincidences don't stop there but elaboration will have to wait until Norman is ready. I am beginning to feel that my part in this is that of a 'sorting office'.

For you, the reader, this may have been a journey of a different kind, and what has been presented in this book, may be further support for your own ideas and beliefs. To the reader who has had experiences of an 'unusual' nature, I hope has found this book useful, either by way of approach or simply by 'shaking it all up' and looking at what falls where. For example, I have indicated that my mathematical ability is not really been adequate for solving some problems herein, and 'the old grey matter' has been shaken up a bit but numbers can expose patterns if present. On the other hand I have had a brief glimpse of another kind of dimension, a non-mathematical dimension. Let me give you a morsel to whet your appetite. Take my full name count and Norman's, 182 and 374 and make, say, block diagrams.

There are several observations that can be made, but I will mention one and leave you work out others if you so wish. Perform a mirror image on the second (Norman's) diagram so that we have –

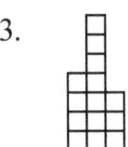

add it to the first diagram using the same base of 3 as above –

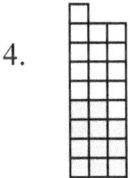

However, the lower 3 by 3 in 3. & 4. cancel each other leaving 5 – now revert to original image.

Count the block number in the columns to convert to our number system and the answer is 556, which is of course, the total count for both our name counts. This is a simplified version of some of the diagrams I have used in my study, which I believe is at a very elementary stage. Nonetheless, although Mi stated that Mi life does not use numbers, what I have given above might represent a route by which Mi could convert to, or perhaps more likely, study our number system. Be that as it may, it does not take a genius to see the above diagrams may have some computer-related analogy, Pixels.

The newspaper *The Guardian* ran an article on February 12th 2005 concerning the amazing mathematical talents of a 26-year old man who is autistic. I will not recall the whole article but just the portion that is of interest here. The scientist involved says – "Actually, he isn't 'calculating': there is nothing conscious about what he is doing. He arrives at the answer instantly. Since his epileptic fit, he has been able to see numbers as shapes, colours and textures. The number two, for instance, is a motion, and five is a clap of thunder."

"When I multiply numbers together, I see two shapes. The image starts to change and evolve, and a third shape emerges. That's the answer. It's mental imagery. It's like maths without having to think."

Therefore, perhaps Mi's ideas about interacting with our environment are not so far fetched after all, and it is possible to live in a numberless world. For us Human Beings however, being autistic might be a high price to pay.

Finally, I think I should give a little encouragement to the Human Race. Have we really done, or have behaved, as badly, or inefficiently as some accounts indicate. If the theory of evolution is valid then human life is still in its infancy. On the other hand, if we are the product of an experiment or perhaps the seed of some other extra terrestrial race or development, then perhaps the blame is not entirely our own. The mythical arguments for life here on Earth are well known, and though I don't wish to debate that subject here, you have read herein that both Norman and I have studied certain facets of such an idea. I hasten to add that the main concern in this study was with 'gods' as opposed a single divine entity, but then 'Jehovah' = 69, and sixty nine plus ninety six equals one hundred and sixty five; 165 divided by Tridel is equal to the count for 'gods'.

I personally feel that Mi wanted to teach us something; I have been enlightened to some other ideas but it may be that if Mi felt that some degree of success had been achieved with Norman and me, then the entity might pay someone else a more extensive visit.

What do you think?

*

Bottom page 154
14+7+3+1+0+6+8+13+7+7 = 66

Second paragraph page 165
144+21+6+36=144+63 = 207

'My reply' page 168/169

1. Sequential addition for the date 12/2/1943 = 28 and 12/8/1983 = 32. Number of days to Aug.12 = 224, 224÷28 = 8, 224÷32 = 7, 7+8 = 15 = 6. Years – 40÷6 = 3+11÷3 (Tridel plus 3 = 6.66666…)

2. The total number of days in forty years 40×365.25 = 14610

3.   14610÷374 (Norman's name count) = 39.064 (count for Enki?).

4. But 14610-(39[Enki]×374 = 24

Bottom page 170 – ice & water etc.

67+76 = 143, 17+71 = 88, 58+85 = 143, 38+83 = 121

Subtracting 'ice' from 'water', 143-88 = 55; adding them all together 143+88+143+121+55 = 550. 'Ocean' had already been considered and both 'water' and 'steam' give identical mirror image totals of 143 so again 143-88 = 55.

--------Epilogue-------

*

Top of page 171
(67+76)+(38+83)+(55+55) = 374

Third paragraph page 173
Mena equals 1-2-2-1, and the number 1221 is exactly equal to Norman's full name count times 2 plus the mirror image, 748 plus 473: or 1221 divided by Tridel then add 'Mira' equals 374. Again, 1221 divided by Tridel then add 'Lawrencium' (119), take away 'Mira Ceti' (78) and the answer is 374 Norman's name count. 374+119+22-(1221÷ Tridel) = my name count, 182.

Book references

Gods, Demons and Symbols of Ancient Mesopotamia. An Illustrated Dictionary. Jeremy Black and Anthony Green ISBN 0-292-70794-0

The Montauk Project by Preston B. Nichols with Peter Moon, Sky Books, ISBN 0-9631889-0-9

The Montauk Revisited by Preston B. Nichols and Peter Moon, Sky Books, ISBN 0-9631889-1-7

The Music of Time by Preston B. Nichols with Peter Moon, Sky Books, ISBN 0-9678162-0-3

The Philadelphia Experiment by Charles Berlitz, ISBN 0-285-62999-9

Sumerian Mythology revised edition. A study of Spiritual and Literary Achievement in the Third Millenium B.C. Samuel Noah Kramer. ISBN 0-8122-1047-6

www.ingramcontent.com/pod-product-compliance
Lightning Source LLC
Chambersburg PA
CBHW060504290526
45791CB00001B/258